fitness food

fitness food

The essential guide to eating well and performing better

Introductory text by
Dr S Holt (PhD, dietitian)

MURDOCH BOOKS

contents

DISCLAIMER

The aim of this book is to provide healthy adults with valid advice about good eating habits to fuel physical activity and maintain good health. The book contains recipes that are consistent with this advice. This information is not intended to replace any advice about diet and exercise that has been given to you by a health professional. If you have a health condition that requires medical treatment, it is important that you consult your doctor before making any changes to your diet or physical activity program. The dietary information may not be applicable to elite athletes because they are able to exercise at much greater intensities than non-elite sportspeople. Therefore, athletes training to compete at a high level would benefit from consulting a sports dietitian for individually tailored dietary advice.

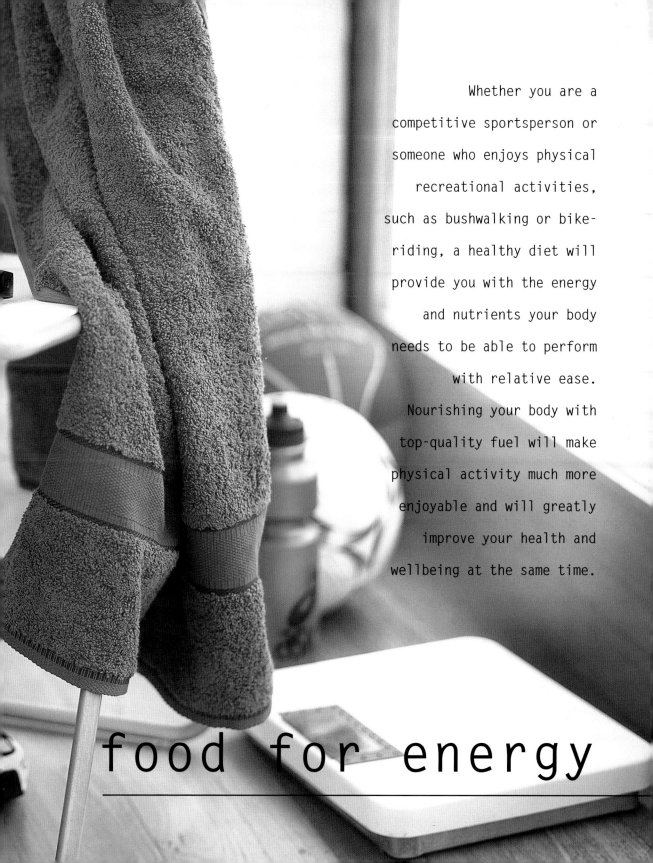

Whether you are a competitive sportsperson or someone who enjoys physical recreational activities, such as bushwalking or bike-riding, a healthy diet will provide you with the energy and nutrients your body needs to be able to perform with relative ease. Nourishing your body with top-quality fuel will make physical activity much more enjoyable and will greatly improve your health and wellbeing at the same time.

food for energy

live the healthy life: eat well, be active and feel great

Many of us exercise to stay fit and healthy, while others make a living through physical work or competitive sport. One thing that all active people have in common is the need for a healthy, varied diet. This provides the energy and nutrients for our bodies to be able to perform and recover from physical activity and stay healthy in the long term.

The type of foods that you eat on a regular basis will affect your ability to perform both physically and mentally, as well as your sense of vitality and wellbeing. If you exercise regularly but fail to eat a healthy diet, your body won't perform as well as it could, and you may even give up regular exercise altogether because it feels so difficult.

If long-term health is not your immediate concern, and you only exercise because you enjoy the thrill of competitive sport, good nutrition should still be part of your daily training program, because, without it, you'll never reach your full potential. The bottom line is that you won't reap all the benefits of the time you've invested in exercising or training if you don't nourish your body with healthy foods and give it quality fuel to run on.

The nutritional analysis of all recipes has been calculated using the metric system; this is the system preferred by the scientific community because of its accuracy, particularly for small measures. Even if you are unfamiliar with the metric system, you can use the nutritional information as a guide by comparing it to the recommended daily requirements given in the introductory tables and working out what proportion of your daily intake the meal contains. However, if you prefer, the following equations can help you convert to imperial. To convert grams to ounces, multiply by 0.035. To convert kilograms to pounds, multiply by 2.2046.

the dietary game plan The information in this book is intended to provide healthy active people with guidelines about the best dietary habits to keep you fit and healthy so you can keep exercising regularly. The more exercise you do, the more energy, nutrients and fluid you need to power your activities and keep your body in good working order. If you exercise at a low intensity, such as doing yoga, Pilates, light aerobics or walking, then the guidelines discussed in this book for lower-fat eating and an adequate fluid intake still apply to you. The nutrition information discussed in this book for more intense physical training and competitive sports events may not be relevant to you. However, the healthy recipes in this book have been chosen to cater for everyone's energy needs.

Whether you're a serious athlete or a recreational exerciser, you are not going to enjoy exercise or get the most out of your training sessions if you don't feel energized. Your body needs a wide range of nutrients, plenty of water and adequate rest to enable it to quickly produce energy.

Good nutrition requires long-term attention, because there is no magic food or supplement that can be taken before an event to produce a winning performance. It is actually your regular 'everyday' diet that has the biggest influence on your physical performance during an event. You may train for many hours each week for sports events that last only for 15–20 minutes, just so you can perform the physical and mental actions required with relative ease. Much more of your time will be spent in training than in competition and, therefore, your training diet has a greater capacity to affect your performance. This applies to competitive athletes, as well as those who participate in vigorous activities such as hiking, mountain-biking or long fishing trips. The quality of your everyday diet will affect how energetic you feel during these activities, as well as your stamina.

If your diet is less than nutritious on a regular basis, then you may become deficient in certain nutrients, such as iron or calcium, which can directly impair your ability to perform physical activity or recover from training and injuries. Although the exact amount of nutrients you need depends on your gender, age and activity level, the same guidelines for an optimal fitness diet apply to all healthy adults. Apart from the extra carbohydrate and fluid needed, the dietary guidelines for sportspeople are the same as those given to active people who want to maintain good health. You may need to make these dietary goals a priority in your life, just as you focus on setting aside time for regular physical activity. It takes commitment, knowledge and organization. This book will give you suggestions about how to easily incorporate these healthy eating patterns into your busy life.

carbohydrates — foods for energy

Just as a car engine runs on energy from petrol, the human body runs on the energy it obtains from the nutrients in the diet and from its own nutrient stores. The carbohydrates (sugars and starches) that we consume are the main source of fuel that powers our brain and exercising muscles.

After carbohydrate is eaten and digested, any that is not immediately needed for fuel is stored in the liver and muscles as glycogen. This stored carbohydrate can be quickly broken down at times when the body needs more energy, such as in between meals and during exercise, to provide the body with readily available fuel. Unlike the body's fat stores, which are very large and could fuel many days of walking, the body's glycogen stores are relatively small and can usually fuel only a few hours of continuous exercise. They are also constantly being used, so we need to refill them by regularly eating carbohydrate. In contrast, the body's fat stores are so large that any fat

When working out your intake (see table right), take care not to overestimate your true carbohydrate needs to prevent weight gain. Body weight refers to a healthy body weight for your height. The activity levels include the intensity and the duration of an activity, and the times refer to the amount of time you are actually being active. If you are more muscular and train more intensely you should use the higher carbohydrate intake for your activity level. If you are less muscular and do not train intensely you should use the lower carbohydrate value for your activity level.

HOW MUCH CARBOHYDRATE DO I NEED EACH DAY?

PHYSICAL ACTIVITY LEVEL	RECOMMENDED DAILY CARBOHYDRATE INTAKE *
Light activity: **less than 1 hour per day** Walking, easy swimming or cycling, low-impact aerobics	4–5
Light to moderate activity: **1 hour per day** Easy jogging, moderate aerobics, social sports	5–6
Moderate activity: **1–2 hours per day** 1-hour run, training for sports such as football, basketball, squash	6–7
Moderate to heavy activity: **2–4 hours per day** Serious training for high-level competitive sports (swimming, tennis, distance running, football)	7–8
Heavy activity: **more than 4 hours per day** Continuous intense activity such as training for ironman events, marathon running or swimming, Olympic distance triathlon	8–10

* grams of carbohydrate per kg body weight per day.
Source: Pocket Guide to the GI Factor and Sports Nutrition *by Helen O'Connor, Jennie Brand-Miller, Stephen Colaguiri & Kaye Foster-Powell, Hodder & Stoughton, 1999.*

that is used during exercise doesn't significantly decrease the total amount of fat stored in the body. Body fat is broken down into fuel at a much slower rate than glycogen and is basically a supplementary fuel to carbohydrate for the first 90–120 minutes of exercise, after which the body's glycogen stores begin to deplete. At this point, athletes will fight a growing battle with fatigue, as fat, a more slowly available fuel, becomes the main power source. Endurance athletes refer to the feeling they experience when their body becomes depleted of carbohydrate as 'hitting the wall', which is a gruelling and unpleasant sensation. However, fatigue caused by carbohydrate depletion can be prevented or reduced by consuming carbohydrate during endurance events and by eating a high-carbohydrate diet before the event to increase the body's glycogen stores.

Regardless of whether you are an elite athlete or a recreational exerciser, if you don't eat enough carbohydrate on a regular basis, you'll feel less energetic and will tire more quickly during exercise. The more exercise you do, the more carbohydrate you need to eat each day (see table on page 10). If you train intensely every day, ensure your meals and snacks are based on carbohydrate-rich foods so you replenish your glycogen levels in between training sessions. The physical and mental demands of training are already tiring, so it is important that your diet re-energizes you.

Health authorities recommend that at least 55 per cent of your daily energy (kilojoules) intake should come from carbohydrate. This is suitable for people who do under an hour of exercise each day or those who exercise for longer but at a low intensity, such as 90 minutes of walking. Serious sportspeople who have heavy training sessions may need to get 60–70 per cent of their daily energy intake from carbohydrate (400–700 g per day).

power of the pyramid Make sure your carbohydrate comes from a wide range of wholesome foods, because certain vitamins and minerals are required by the body to convert carbohydrates into energy. Many convenience foods contain plenty of carbohydrate, but they may also contain too much fat or not enough vitamins and minerals. Given that many people obtain less than 50 per cent of their energy from carbohydrates, you will need to make some dietary changes to decrease your fat intake and to eat more nutritious carbohydrate-rich foods. The healthy diet pyramid approach (see page 247), where meals and snacks are based on grain products, legumes, fruit and vegetables, is the easiest model to use. This means that two-thirds of each meal you eat should come from a combination of grain products, legumes, fruit or vegetables. It's also important to vary these foods in your diet to get the full range of vitamins and minerals. For advice on the amount of carbohydrate you should be eating, see a sports dietitian.

Some carbohydrates are broken down at a much faster rate than others. These rapidly digested carbohydrates can produce a higher and faster rise in your blood sugar level than some sugary foods. The Glycaemic Index (GI) is a ranking of foods according to how they affect blood sugar levels. Low-GI foods (slowly digested) are best for most people because they help you to eat less as you feel fuller for longer; they also help you to control your blood sugar levels. Most of the recipes in this book are low and medium GI.

CARBOHYDRATE-RICH FOODS

• *Bread, bread rolls, bagels, crumpets, English muffins (preferably wholegrain)*

• *Breakfast cereals, natural muesli, porridge, semolina, breakfast cereal bars*

• *Pasta, noodles, couscous, polenta, rice, barley and other grains*

• *Fruit: fresh, frozen, tinned in natural juice, dried*

• *Starchy vegetables: potatoes, sweet potatoes, corn, pumpkin*

• *Legumes: lentils, chickpeas, baked beans, kidney beans*

• *Low-fat bakery products: pancakes, pikelets, muffins*

• *Low-fat dairy products: yoghurt, smoothies, custard, flavoured milk*

fat — dietary and body

A small amount of fat is necessary for good health, but many of us eat far more than we need, which can lead to weight gain and an increased risk of developing heart disease, diabetes as well as some cancers. For sportspeople, a high-fat diet is undesirable, because it can increase the amount of fat stored in the body and is usually accompanied by an inadequate carbohydrate intake, both of which can directly impair physical performance. Fats contain twice as many kilojoules as carbohydrate or protein. Therefore, relatively small amounts of fatty foods contain a lot of energy and can be a source of weight gain.

Studies have shown that fatty foods are generally not as filling as those rich in protein or carbohydrate, and can also reduce how alert you feel, so it makes sense to make some simple changes such as switching from full-fat to low-fat dairy products and using low-fat cooking methods to reduce your fat intake. You can actually eat more food on a low-fat diet based on the healthy diet pyramid (see page 247) and still be eating fewer kilojoules than if you were eating a high-fat diet.

For many sports, a relatively low body-fat level can help athletes perform at the best of their ability, because the athlete will have less dead weight (non-muscular tissue) to move around. However, before you embark on a fat-loss program, it's important to determine whether you really need to lose any weight and whether the methods you want to adopt are healthy in the long run. Have your body-fat level measured by a health professional.

If you are technically overweight, then losing some body fat by making healthy changes to your diet and exercise programs can help improve your health and your performance. However, if you strive to achieve a body-fat level that is unnaturally low for you, using excessive exercise and/or very strict dieting, you will eventually compromise your sporting ability and your health.

Women should remember that they need a certain amount of body fat in order to remain fertile, and this level varies between women. In females who diet and exercise so much that their body fat goes below its natural limit, hormonal changes will occur that increase the risk of developing stress fractures and osteoporosis. Men and women who are trying to control their weight with strict eating and exercise also run the risk of developing long-term disordered eating. If you are struggling to control your weight so you can meet a certain weight category for your sport, you may need to consider moving to a higher weight category or changing to a different sport that doesn't have weight limitations. If you are a non-professional athlete, you should be participating in a sport for good health and enjoyment.

FATS IN FOOD

• *Saturated fats are mainly derived from the fat in animal products, such as dairy foods, eggs, meats and poultry. It is also found in coconut and palm oils and foods made with these oils. Eating too much saturated fat can increase your blood cholesterol level.*

• *Monounsaturated fats are found in olive and canola oils and margarines made from these oils, avocados and some nuts. It can help lower your blood cholesterol level if eaten as part of a diet that's low in total fat and saturated fat.*

• *Polyunsaturated fats are found in good amounts in nuts, seeds, some fish and vegetable oils. They can also lower your blood cholesterol level if eaten as part of a diet that is low in total fat and saturated fat.*

HOW MUCH FAT DO I NEED?

CATEGORY	APPROXIMATE DAILY FAT REQUIREMENT (grams of fat per day)
Weight loss	25–40
Sedentary women	30–50
Sedentary men	40–60
Active women	40–70
Active men	50–80
Endurance athletes undertaking 2–4 hours of heavy training per day	
Men	80–100
Women	50–80

Source: Sports Nutrition Basics *by Helen O'Connor and Donna Hay,*
JB Fairfax Press, Sydney, 1998.

ESSENTIAL FATTY ACIDS

Omega-3 and omega-6 essential fatty acids are polyunsaturated fats that can't be made by the body. This means that they must be obtained from the diet. An imbalanced intake of these oils is thought to exacaberate some conditions such as inflammation, blood clotting and heart disease.

• Omega-3 fats are found in linseeds, walnuts, canola oil, fish oils, soya beans and fatty fish such as salmon, tuna, trout, trevally and mackerel.

• Omega-6 fats are found in sunflower, safflower, soya bean, peanut and sesame oils.

healthy low-fat eating for physical fitness Regular exercise, together with a low-fat diet, is an excellent way to keep your body- fat level under control and make sure that carbohydrate is the main fuel in your diet. You just need to focus on getting the right amount of good-quality fat from wholesome food, such as nuts, seeds, avocados, fish and lean meat, while cutting back on less nutritious fatty food, like chips and biscuits.

Start your low-fat eating plan by making one or two changes at a time, then stick with them until they feel natural, rather than trying to do everything at once. For example, you could first switch from using full-fat to reduced-fat dairy products for a few weeks, then switch to low-fat versions. You may initially miss the creamy mouth-feel of full-fat dairy products, but after a few weeks you'll find that you no longer enjoy their fatty taste.

how much fat should I be eating? The amount of fat you need each day depends on your gender, your healthy weight range, and your activity level. Use the table above to determine the total amount of fat that health professionals recommend you should aim to consume each day. In general, if you are short in stature or have a slim build, the smaller numerals on the table apply to you.

protein

Dietary proteins or, more specifically, the amino acids that make up different proteins, are needed by the body for tissue growth, maintenance and repair, as well as for producing antibodies and the enzymes and hormones that regulate many important metabolic processes. Some amino acids can also be used as fuel when carbohydrate and fat supplies are low. Although protein has many vital functions, the amount of protein you need to eat each day is relatively small, because, unlike carbohydrate, large amounts of protein are not burnt for fuel. Most protein comes from animal products such as dairy, meat, poultry and seafood.

The protein in our muscles is constantly undergoing remodelling—being repaired or remade as it is injured or ages. Some of the protein that is broken down is reused by the body, while the remainder must come from the diet. Studies have shown that regular exercise increases the amount of protein needed by the body, mostly to repair tissues and grow extra muscle.

HOW MUCH PROTEIN DO I NEED?

PHYSICAL ACTIVITY LEVEL	RECOMMENDED DAILY PROTEIN INTAKE *	
	Males	Females
Non-active, sedentary people	0.8	0.8
General sports activity (light–moderate)	1.0	1.0
Teenage and growing athletes	2.0	2.0
Endurance athletes *Recreational* *Moderate intensity* *Elite (moderate training)* *Elite (intense, heavy training)*	 0.85 1.2 1.6 2.0	 0.84 0.9 1.2 1.7
Strength athletes *Untrained, beginning weight-training program* *Trained*	 1.7 1.2	 1.3 0.9

* grams of protein per kg body weight per day

Sources: The Complete Guide to Food for Sports Performance, *by Dr L Burke, Allen & Unwin, 1995;* Sports Nutrition Basics, *by H O'Connor & D Hay, JB Fairfax Press, 1998.*

In general, the longer and more intense your regular training sessions are, the more protein you will need from your diet (see table on page 14).

Active people who do need to check that their protein intake is adequate include serious endurance and strength athletes who complete long, intense daily training sessions; vegetarians; teenagers who are still growing; very restrictive eaters; and pregnant and breast-feeding women. However, most of us already eat more protein than we need and may be able to improve our sporting performance by eating more nutritious carbohydrate-rich foods instead of more protein. Many active people already eat more food than non-active people, and this extra food typically provides them with the extra protein they need.

To get the most out of your body, you need to give it the best-quality fuel, so focus on getting protein from a wide range of wholesome foods, such as lean red meat and poultry, fish and seafood, eggs, low-fat dairy products, nuts, seeds and legumes. This will help limit your saturated-fat intake and provide you with a range of vitamins and minerals.

Dietary proteins are made up of chains of amino acids, and there are about 20 different amino acids commonly found in foods. Eleven of these amino acids can be made in the human body (non-essential amino acids). The other nine (essential amino acids) can't be made in adult bodies and so must come from the diet. Protein from lean animal foods, such as red meat, fish, eggs and low-fat dairy products, contain all of the essential amino acids needed by the human body. If your diet doesn't provide all the essential amino acids it needs, your body will get them by breaking down some of its own proteins, which may compromise your muscle strength and performance. Plant foods usually contain incomplete proteins that lack some essential amino acids. However, it's possible for vegetarians to get all the amino acids by combining foods from different groups, such as dairy products with grain products or legumes, or legumes with grains. Vegetarians who eat eggs and dairy foods usually get all the essential amino acids they need, but vegans will have to work harder to make sure that their meals are well balanced and nutritious and contain adequate protein, vitamins and minerals.

myths about big muscles Many people believe that protein-rich foods and protein supplements will increase their muscle size and strength. However, the truth is that your ability to increase your muscle size depends on your genes and whether you follow the right type of training program and diet. You can't get your muscles to grow just by eating more protein or taking protein supplements. You need to stimulate your muscles with

appropriate resistance-training exercise that becomes progressively more challenging over time. For advice about an appropriate weight-training program, consult a qualified fitness professional. It's important too that your diet contains adequate energy, primarily from carbohydrate. You need to fuel your muscles with carbohydrate so you can do the required weight-training exercise that is needed to stimulate them to grow. Protein needs are increased by weight training but not to a large degree (1.2–2 g protein per kg body weight per day). Eating more protein than your body needs will not make your muscles grow bigger; instead it can increase your body fat level. You are likely to make greater gains in improving your strength and sports performance by investing in wholesome foods and professional personal training sessions rather than buying protein supplements.

get muscle mass the healthy way Increasing your food intake as part of a strength-training program can be difficult if you have a busy lifestyle. Make sure that you stock your fridge and pantry with appropriate foods and carry healthy snacks with you during the day, so you always have suitable food available. Rather than trying to increase the amount of food you eat at main meals, you may need to eat more frequently during the day. In fact, spreading your protein intake over the day, by including some protein-rich food (such as milk on cereal, yoghurt, lean meat or low-fat cheese on a sandwich) at each meal and snack may improve muscle-mass gains by keeping amino acids circulating in your bloodstream. Muscle growth, in response to exercise, is stimulated in the presence of an adequate amino acid supply. Compact, low-fat snacks and drinks are a good way to boost your carbohydrate and protein intakes during the day without reducing your appetite for main meals. There are lots of snacks to choose from—fruit smoothies, milkshakes, liquid meal supplements, yoghurt, dried fruit, ham and salad sandwiches, power bars and breakfast cereal bars.

Studies have shown that you may be able to increase your muscle mass with regular weight training if you eat a snack that is rich in carbohydrate with a moderate amount of protein (1 g of carbohydrate per kg of your body weight plus 7–10 g of protein) either before your weight-training session or within 30 minutes of finishing your training session.

The amount of food that is required for this high-carb snack will vary according to your body weight. You can use the information on food labels to help you work out how much food you need or you can see a sports dietitian for advice about the specific quantities and types of food that are suitable for your training purposes.

iron

An adequate iron intake is essential for achieving optimal physical performance. Iron is needed for a healthy immune system, for producing energy from the nutrients you eat, and for the production of haemoglobin (the molecule that carries oxygen in the bloodstream to the body's tissues) and myoglobin (the molecule that stores oxygen in muscles for use during exercise). Many people do not get enough iron from their diet on a regular basis, and iron deficiency is a common nutritional problem.

Symptoms of iron deficiency include chronic tiredness; impaired mood and mental functioning; decreased tolerance to cold; shortness of breath with less physical exertion; greater difficulty in performing and recovering from exercise. These symptoms could also be caused by factors other than a low iron intake, such as over-training, inadequate intakes of carbohydrate and protein, or a virus. Therefore, it's vital you see a doctor to have a check-up and blood test to ensure that you really are iron-deficient before you decide to take iron supplements. Problems can arise if you take these supplements when you don't need them, particularly over a long period of time.

Iron deficiency progresses towards anaemia through a series of stages if a person's iron intake continues to be inadequate. As the body's iron stores continue to drop, more physiological problems arise and symptoms become more debilitating. Anaemia occurs when the body's iron stores are completely depleted and the blood's haemoglobin level is below normal. At this point, your ability to perform any physical activity is greatly reduced, and even walking up a flight of stairs can feel like climbing a small mountain. Not everyone with iron deficiency has anaemia, but you will keep progressing towards it if you don't increase the amount of iron in your diet.

If you are active you may need more iron than a sedentary person, particularly if you sweat heavily and do high-impact exercise, such as prolonged running and jumping. Heavy exercisers may also absorb less iron during the day. Women are at greater risk of iron deficiency than men due to menstruation, and the risk is increased if they restrict their food intake.

dietary sources of iron   Iron is found in plant and animal foods, but it occurs in two different chemical forms: haem and non-haem iron. Most of the iron in animal foods is in the haem form, which is the same kind of iron that's found in the human body. Most of the iron in plant foods is in the non-haem form. Haem iron is absorbed far more efficiently into the human body than non-haem iron. Good sources of this type of iron include lean red meat, liver, darker poultry meat, mussels, tuna and sardines. Good sources of

TIPS FOR INCREASING YOUR IRON INTAKE

• *Include a palm-sized portion of lean red meat or liver in your diet at least 3–5 times a week. Add slices of lean meat to sandwiches.*

• *Read the nutrition information on breakfast cereal boxes to help you choose iron-enriched cereals. However, don't regularly eat bran-based breakfast cereals, if you're iron-deficient as bran inhibits the absorption of iron.*

• *Look for ways to combine foods containing vitamin C with those containing non-haem iron, such as adding parsley and tomatoes to omelettes, fruit or fruit juice with cereal and kidney beans to meat dishes.*

• *Drink tea and coffee in between meals rather than with meals because chemicals in these drinks decrease iron absorption.*

• Eat calcium-rich foods for snacks and desserts, such as yoghurt, low-fat ice cream, sardines on toast, banana smoothies, low-fat custard, low-fat macaroni cheese.

• Use reduced- or low-fat cheese on bread instead of butter or margarine.

• If you're lactose-intolerant, try to eat small amounts of dairy products—most cheeses don't contain very much lactose. You can also use calcium-enriched soy milk or lactose-reduced milk.

• Read the nutrition information panel on food labels to compare the calcium contents of different products. Look for calcium-enriched milk, drink powders and breakfast cereals.

• Limit your alcohol intake to no more than two standard drinks a day with some alcohol-free days each week.

• Don't smoke.

• Limit your salt intake, don't add salt to your meals and look for reduced-salt products.

• Limit your intake of caffeine and cola drinks.

• Women shouldn't lose so much body fat that they stop menstruating.

non-haem iron include iron-enriched breakfast cereals and drink powders, eggs, legumes, seeds, wheat germ, oat bran, tofu, dried fruit, broccoli and spinach. It's possible to increase the amount of non-haem iron you absorb by consuming it together with animal foods that contain haem iron or foods rich in vitamin C such as orange juice, capsicum (pepper), strawberries, kiwifruit, broccoli, Brussels sprouts or red cabbage. A good combination for breakfast is an iron-enriched breakfast cereal plus milk, fresh kiwi fruit and orange juice; and for lunch or dinner, stir-fried meat, mixed vegetables and rice.

calcium

Calcium is needed, together with phosphorus and other nutrients, to maintain the strength of our bones and teeth. It is also needed to regulate blood pressure and blood clotting, and for muscles and nerves to function normally. Bone is a living tissue that is constantly being broken down and reformed. It acts as a reservoir from which the body draws calcium for important metabolic processes when levels are relatively low. Consequently, if we don't have sufficient calcium in our diet it can cause the bones to become brittle later on in life. Our bones have usually stopped growing in length by the time we are 18 years old, but they can continue to grow in strength up until our early thirties. Between 18 and 30 years of age, our bones will have reached their peak bone mass (size and strength), which is determined by our genes, diet and the amount of exercise we do. Between the ages of 35 and 45 years, bone begins to break down at a faster rate than it is rebuilt and, over time, this can lead to osteoporosis, where the bones have become so weak that they fracture more easily.

Many children and adults eat less calcium than is recommended by health authorities, which puts them at greater risk of developing osteoporosis as they get older. Women also have a greater risk of developing osteoporosis than men because of their smaller bone mass. They also have a faster rate of bone loss after menopause, caused by a drop in the body's oestrogen level. Young girls who exercise intensely and restrict their food intake also have an increased risk of developing osteoporosis. This is because they can lose so much body fat that they develop amenorrhoea—they stop menstruating regularly (they have less than four cycles a year) or they don't start menstruating at all. Amenorrhoea is accompanied by a lower oestrogen level, which means that the bone is more susceptible to calcium loss. Although many young women would still prefer to be lean now and worry about the consequences later, prolonged amenorrhoea together with high-impact exercise increases their risk of developing stress fractures in the near

CATEGORY	RECOMMENDED DAILY CALCIUM INTAKE *	
	Males	Females
Teenagers, 16–18 years	1000	800
Adults, 19–54 years	800	800
Adults, over 54 years	800	1000 *(from menopause onwards)*
Amenorrhoeic females	N/A	1000
Pregnant women	N/A	1100
Breast-feeding women	N/A	1200

HOW MUCH CALCIUM DO I NEED?

* *milligrams of calcium per day. Source: Recommended Dietary Intakes for Use in Australia. National Health and Medical Research Council, Australia, 1991.*

future. Bone loss caused by amenorrhoea can generally be reversed if a woman gains weight and starts menstruating regularly again by nourishing herself with a healthy, calcium-rich diet. However, it not yet known whether the repaired bone will be as strong as the original. See your doctor if your menstrual cycle has been irregular for more than six months.

dietary sources of calcium Dairy products such as milk, yoghurt and cheese are the richest sources of calcium, and they also contain the other essential nutrients needed for strong, healthy bones (protein, phosphorus and magnesium). The lactose sugar in milk enhances calcium absorption in the body. Just three normal serves of dairy products each day supplies most of the daily recommended amount of calcium for healthy people (one serve is equal to 200 g (7 oz) yoghurt; 250 ml (7 fl oz) milk; two thin slices of reduced-fat cheese). Some dairy products, such as low-fat milk, are also fortified with extra calcium and are excellent choices for active people. Other sources of calcium include calcium-enriched soy milk and tofu; salmon and sardines, tinned in brine or water and eaten with their bones; oysters; crab; prawns (shrimp); mussels; calcium-enriched breakfast cereals and drink powders; tahini, almonds with their skin; Brazil nuts; and dried figs. However, the calcium in non-dairy foods is generally less well absorbed, because some

plant food components, such as fibre, tannins and oxalates, reduce the amount of calcium absorbed by the body. Vegans and others who do not eat dairy products must work much harder to make sure that they regularly get adequate calcium from other foods in their diet. They would benefit from seeing a dietitian for advice about balancing their diet and whether a calcium supplement is needed. A calcium supplement should not be used in place of a healthy balanced diet, if at all possible.

antioxidants

Regular exercise produces many health benefits, but it also naturally causes an increased production of free radicals in the body. These highly reactive unstable molecules can cause oxidative damage to cell membranes. Research studies have shown that the increased free radical production following intense or prolonged exercise can contribute to muscle fatigue during endurance events or exacerbate muscle injury, particularly if you are untrained. However, there is no good evidence from studies to suggest that antioxidant supplements can delay the onset of fatigue, prevent injury or improve sports performance—even in addition to a healthy diet. In fact, the regular consumption of antioxidant supplements may have potentially harmful side effects.

Many foods, particularly fruits, herbs and vegetables, are naturally rich in antioxidants. Naturally occurring nutrients in foods that have antioxidant effects include vitamin C, vitamin E, beta-carotene (pro-vitamin A), flavonoids, manganese and selenium. If you regularly eat a carbohydrate-rich diet that's based on wholegrain products, legumes, fresh fruit and vegetables, with moderate amounts of lean protein-rich foods, it will benefit your health and your sports performance to a greater extent than antioxidant supplements taken with a less-than-ideal diet or less varied and nutritious diet.

fluid

Water accounts for 50–70 per cent of our body weight and has many vital functions. The body can't store water, and therefore, a regular fluid intake throughout the day is essential to replace the fluid that's continually being lost from the body. At rest, an average adult generally loses 1–2 litres (35–70 fl oz) of water, depending on the temperature of their environment and the size of their body. The body loses even more water in hot, dry environments and during strenuous physical activity. As you intensify your exercise, the heat production in the body rises. The evaporation of sweat from the body helps to reduce this heat and prevent the body from overheating. If you don't drink enough fluid to replace the fluid lost from your body, you will become dehydrated and run the risk of developing heatstroke.

Dehydration is one of the most common but preventable nutritional problems that adversely affects performances in all types and levels of competitive sport and recreational activities. Common symptoms of mild dehydration include headaches, cramps, fatigue and dizziness. A loss of just two per cent of your body weight from water (mild dehydration) lowers your blood volume, reduces the amount of heat you can lose by sweating and reduces your capacity to perform mental and physical activities—even if you don't feel badly affected. Thirst, unfortunately, is not a good indication of your body's fluid needs, because you're already somewhat dehydrated by the time you actually feel thirsty. Therefore, it is important to prevent dehydration by drinking plenty of fluid before you feel thirsty. Try to get into the habit of drinking water regularly throughout the day. Also, take a water bottle with you when you go out and have bottled water on hand at work or school, to you can drink regularly during the day.

To avoid dehydration during exercise you need to drink plenty of water before you start, then drink small amounts during the session, and afterwards drink enough to fully replace what you lost while exercising. At least 30 minutes before you start exercising, drink 2–3 glasses of water to top up your fluid level. Do this gradually rather than drinking a large amount just before you start. During exercise, sip water whenever a drinking opportunity arises. You need 150–300 ml (5–10½ fl oz) of fluid every 15–20 minutes, depending on the temperature and your sweat rate. Practise drinking sufficient water during your training sessions, so you become used to exercising while you're fully hydrated. Don't try it for the first time during an important event in case you get an over-full stomach or bladder. If you're training for a team sport, ask the coach to set aside time for drink breaks.

restore the balance After exercise, you need to drink 1.5 times the amount of fluid you lost within 1–2 hours of completing the exercise, in order to restore your body's fluid balance. For example, if you're 1 kg (2 lb 4 oz) lighter after finishing a heavy training session, you need to drink 1.5 litres (52 fl oz) of fluid. You should begin drinking water soon after you finish exercising and make water a priority, then continue to drink small amounts of water regularly for the rest of the day, even if you're not thirsty, because you will continue to lose water while your body recovers from the exercise. Avoid alcohol and drinks that contain caffeine after exercise, because they have a diuretic effect and promote fluid loss.

Drinking sufficient water before and during exercise is an easy strategy you can use to improve your sports performance. However, it takes planning and a conscious effort, because many people forget to drink while exercising or find it inconvenient. Research shows that your physical performance will be adversely affected at any level of dehydration, and that you can't get your body to adapt to dehydration by training in a dehydrated state. Look for ways you can increase your fluid consumption during exercise sessions. If you find it hard to drink lots of cold water, then make sure your water bottle is cool but not chilled. If plain water doesn't tempt you to drink, then add a little fruit juice or cordial for flavour, but don't add too much, because high-sugar drinks actually reduce the rate at which your body absorbs water.

alcohol — handle with care Many sportspeople drink alcohol after events, but this is not a healthy practice. After exercise, an athlete's priority should be to help their body recover as much as possible by consuming sufficient water and food. This is particularly important for people who have to exercise again within the next 24 hours. Alcohol is actually a drug or toxin, as far as the body is concerned, and it has a number of undesirable effects that impair the body's ability to recover from exercise. It has a diuretic effect and increases the risk of dehydration. It dilates blood vessels, which can cause fluid to accumulate in damaged tissues and exacerbate injuries.

Alcohol can't be stored in the body. It must be burnt as fuel to prevent it from damaging tissues, which interferes with the metabolic processes that replenish the body's glycogen stores. For these reasons, it is recommended that you avoid alcohol for 24–36 hours after sport, particularly if you've been injured. Sportspeople are not looking after their immediate health

STANDARD SERVES OF ALCOHOL	
DRINK	AMOUNT
Beer—regular (5% alcohol)	¾ regular can (285 ml/10 fl oz)
Beer—light (3% alcohol)	1.2 regular cans (475 ml/16½ fl oz)
Table wines (about 10% alcohol)	1 wine glass (100 ml/3½ fl oz)
Fortified wines (sherry, port) (about 20% alcohol)	1 sherry glass (60 ml/2 fl oz)
Spirits, liqueurs (about 40% alcohol)	1 nip (30 ml/1 fl oz)

needs if they start drinking alcohol after events. Regular alcohol consumption can also be a source of weight gain, because alcoholic beverages contain a lot of energy. Athletes who are trying to control their body fat need to limit their alcohol consumption. When you drink alcohol regularly it increases your body's requirements for B-group vitamins and antioxidants, yet often it displaces nutritious foods from the diet because many people eat less healthy foods when drinking. If you're a member of a sports team that has the habit of drinking alcohol after matches, take drinks and foods with you to events, so you have something healthy on hand instead of alcohol.

As long as you don't consume alcohol before and after exercise, then the moderate consumption of alcohol can be part of a healthy diet. Generally, a moderate intake is defined as no more than 2–4 standard drinks a day for men and no more than 1–2 standard drinks a day for women with some alcohol-free days each week (see table on page 22). People over the age of 65 years are advised to consume only one standard drink a day. A standard drink contains 8–10 g (about ¼ oz) of alcohol. Many large drinking glasses contain more than the standard drink, so use a measuring jug at home to find out what a standard serve of your alcoholic drink looks like in a glass.

the winning edge

What does my body need before an event? The foods and drinks you choose to eat before a sports event can either enhance or impair your performance by determining how energetic and comfortable you feel during the event. However, there are no magic foods or supplements that can counteract months of unhealthy eating or insufficient training before an event. The aim of pre-event meals is to top up your body's glycogen stores (fuel reserves) and fluid levels without making you feel uncomfortable before or during the event. You can start topping up your glycogen stores during the 24–36 hours before an event by consuming low-fat, high-carbohydrate meals and reducing your physical activity.

The night before your event, base your evening meal on high-carbohydrate foods with a small serve of lean protein. You don't need to eat more than usual, because you still have opportunities to eat the following day. You should drink water and carbohydrate-containing fluids, and avoid alcohol, tea, coffee and cola drinks because they have a diuretic effect. It's best to avoid drinking alcohol for at least two days before an event, because it can disturb the muscles' use of carbohydrate for fuel.

On the morning of the event, start the day with a high-carbohydrate breakfast to replace the glycogen your body used during the night. Breakfast

HEALTHY PRE-EVENT MEALS OR SNACKS

• *Breakfast cereal (not toasted muesli) or porridge with low-fat milk and fruit*

• *Toast, crumpets or English muffins with jam, honey or banana*

• *Low-fat pancakes or pikelets with syrup or apple sauce*

• *Low-fat muffins with jam*

• *Fruit salad, stewed or tinned fruit with low-fat yoghurt*

• *High-carbohydrate sports bars or low-fat breakfast cereal bars (not muesli bars or health cakes) and sports drinks*

• *Sandwich or bread roll with jam or banana filling*

• *Pitta bread with low-fat cottage cheese and tomato plus a banana or fruit juice*

• *Pasta with low-fat tomato sauce*

• *Baked or microwaved potato with a low-fat filling*

• *Bread roll and low-fat soup*

• *Tinned spaghetti and toast*

• *Low-fat fruit smoothie*

• *Low-fat rice pudding*

• *Carbohydrate-rich liquid meal drinks*

• Eat low-fat, high-carbohydrate meals and snacks to maximize the body's glycogen stores.

• Drink water at regular intervals, even if you're not thirsty (more than 2 litres/ 70 fl oz per day).

• Limit your fat intake.

• Moderate your protein and fibre intake (concentrate on eating more carbohydrate).

• Limit your intake of salt and caffeine.

• Avoid alcohol.

• Don't eat more food than usual.

• Make sure you have appropriate foods and drinks to take with you to the event.

cereals, fruit, yoghurt, toast or crumpets are good options. If you normally drink tea or coffee, then include this with your meal to avoid any caffeine-withdrawal symptoms, but drink more water to compensate for the diuretic effect of caffeine. If your event is in the morning, you will need to get up early enough so that you can eat breakfast 3–4 hours before you compete. If this is not possible, then you will need to consume a smaller meal or snack and some water 90–120 minutes beforehand. If you're nervous or can't eat much, then try a liquid meal drink, smoothie or a sports bar. If you can't manage to eat very much before your event, then you can use a sports drink during the event for extra fuel. If your event starts later in the afternoon, have breakfast, then lunch or two smaller carbohydrate snacks during the afternoon, leaving 1–2 hours between the last snack and the event.

should I drink water before an event? Yes. You need to drink plenty of water leading up to the event to avoid dehydration. Drink larger volumes of fluid two or more hours before the event, then keep topping up with small sips of water at regular intervals. Take several large water bottles with you, so you have water on hand, as well as suitable food, because good food is often not available at sports venues.

It's important to remember that there is no ideal method of pre-event eating. Your meal pattern on the day of the event depends on the time of your event and your individual food preferences. You should experiment with different types and amounts of foods before your event, so you can find combinations of foods and drinks that leave you feeling adequately full but not uncomfortable during the event.

Don't try new foods or strategies on the day of a competition, in case you get an upset stomach or feel too full or too hungry. Running and other sports that require lots of jumping and running can increase the risk of an upset stomach, so you need to leave yourself enough time before competing to fully digest any food you eat.

Sports drinks or low-fibre and low-fat foods, like white bread with jam or liquid meal supplements, are good choices for people who suffer from nerves and tummy troubles. If you have to compete in several heats or matches on the same day, eat a small light snack or have a sports drink in between to help top up your fuel level and settle a nervous stomach. If you don't have time to eat in between heats or matches, drink a sports drink (about 600 ml/21 fl oz per hour). See a sports dietitian if you would like to develop a precise eating and drinking plan that will keep you well hydrated and fuelled and comfortable during your event.

what does my body need during an event? If you're participating in a sport or event that lasts for 60–90 minutes and you've managed to eat well beforehand, then you only need to drink water during your event. Try to drink small amounts regularly before you become thirsty. Endurance athletes who are exercising intensely for more than 90 minutes may benefit from consuming fluid and some carbohydrate during the event, because they will deplete their carbohydrate stores to some extent in this time. It's important that endurance athletes find out how much food and fluid they can tolerate during an event by practising realistic strategies during training sessions.

Some athletes can tolerate solid food while they're exercising, such as a banana or a power bar, while others can only stomach liquids. You should also think about where you are going to store the food while you're competing. Some triathletes strap a banana to the handlebar of their bike or keep some gummi lollies in a small pocket inside their shorts. In some endurance events, such as triathlons and marathons, drinks and foods are provided by the race organizers, in which case you will need to be comfortable with what's on offer or have a friend stationed at specific locations with your own supplies. You should avoid carbonated and caffeine-containing beverages both during and after exercise.

what does my body need after an event? An athlete's first priority after finishing an event or training is to start drinking lots of water as soon as possible to begin replacing the fluid that was lost during the event. Alcohol should be avoided, particularly if you're injured, because it impairs the body's recovery processes and can make injuries worse by aggravating inflammation. If you want to join your team for a drink after an event, make sure that you first consume all the water and carbohydrate you need before you start drinking any alcoholic beverages. Set yourself a limit of 1–2 drinks only, preferably low-alcohol varieties, or better still, have some mineral water, fruit juice or soft drink (soda), though remember that high-sugar drinks actually reduce the rate at which your body absorbs water.

Serious athletes, who have to train and compete within 12–24 hours of finishing an event, will need to start refilling their carbohydrate stores. You should consume about 50 g (1¾ oz) of carbohydrate within two hours of finishing the event. This is as easy as eating a couple of breakfast cereal bars, three pieces of fruit or drinking 500 ml (17 fl oz) of orange juice. See the list at right for other recovery snack ideas. Following the snack your next main meal should be high in carbohydrate and low in fat. It's a good idea to take suitable foods with you to events so you are well stocked up.

RECOVERY SNACKS CONTAINING 50 G (1¾ oz) OF CARBOHYDRATE

- *825–1000 ml (30–35 fl oz) sports drink*

- *500 ml (17 fl oz) orange juice, soft drink (soda) or flavoured mineral water*

- *2 low-fat breakfast cereal bars*

- *3 pieces of fruit, such as a banana, apple and pear*

- *60 g (2¼ oz) packet of jelly beans or jelly babies*

- *2 x 200 g (7 oz) cartons of low-fat fruit yoghurt*

- *A jam sandwich (2 thick slices of bread with lots of jam and no margarine)*

- *A large bread roll with jam or mashed banana filling*

- *A cup of thick vegetable soup with a large bread roll*

- *A salad sandwich with a slice of lean meat or reduced-fat cheese and a piece of fruit*

- *2 cups of breakfast cereal with low-fat milk*

- *Fresh or tinned fruit salad with low-fat yoghurt*

While you're asleep, your body uses carbohydrate stored in your liver to keep your blood sugar level stable and your vital organs working. The liver's carbohydrate reserve is an important fuel source for exercising muscles during endurance exercise. A carbohydrate-rich breakfast is essential for topping up your body's fuel stores; it will also keep you alert and keep you feeling full and satiated during the morning.

breakfast

marathon muesli

Refill your fuel tanks with this nutritious muesli — rich in carbohydrate, fibre, B-group vitamins, beta-carotene, potassium and magnesium. Add milk for calcium.

30 g (1 oz/⅓ cup) flaked almonds

200 g (7 oz/2 cups) raw rolled oats

60 g (2¼ oz/1 cup) processed bran cereal

40 g (1½ oz/⅓ cup) rye flakes

40 g (1½ oz/¼ cup) pepitas (pumpkin seeds)

2 tbs sunflower seeds

1 tbs linseeds

90 g (3¼ oz/¾ cup) sultanas

185 g (6¼ oz/1 cup) chopped dried apricots

90 g (3¼ oz/½ cup) chopped dried pear

low-fat honey yoghurt or skim milk, to serve

Prep time: 10 minutes

Cooking time: 5 minutes

Serves 6

Preheat the oven to 160°C (315°F/Gas 2–3). Place the almonds on a baking tray in a single layer and toast in the oven for 5 minutes, or until golden. Remove and set aside.

Place the rolled oats, processed bran cereal, rye flakes, pepitas, sunflower seeds and linseeds in a bowl, then stir well to combine. Add the sultanas, apricots and pears as well as the toasted almonds.

Serve with low-fat honey-flavoured yoghurt or skim milk. Keep any remaining muesli in an airtight container for up to 2 weeks.

nutrition per serve Energy 1809 kJ (431 Cal); Fat 11.8 g; Carbohydrate 65.2 g; Protein 10.9 g

bircher muesli

If your regular muesli is a bit ho-hum, try this one. It's not only delicious, it's also rich in carbohydrate and contains most vitamins and minerals.

300 g (10½ oz/3 cups) raw rolled oats

250 ml (9 fl oz/1 cup) low-fat milk

100 g (3½ oz/⅓ cup) low-fat plain yoghurt

100 ml (3½ fl oz) orange juice

3 tbs sugar

125 g (4½ oz/½ cup) low-fat plain yoghurt, extra

2 apples, grated

2 cups mixed seasonal fresh fruit (banana, peach, apricot, melon, apple, strawberries)

honey, to serve

Prep time: 15 minutes + 4 hours refrigeration

Cooking time: Nil

Serves 6

Place the oats, milk, yoghurt, orange juice and sugar in a bowl, and mix together well. Cover and refrigerate for 4 hours, or overnight. Serve with the extra yoghurt, grated apple and fresh fruit of your choice. Drizzle with a little honey, if desired.

variations: You can also add 60 g (2¼ oz/½ cup) slivered almonds, if you like. This will increase the fat and energy content, but the fat will be mostly the unsaturated type.

For extra flavour without adding too many kilojoules, you can add some grated apple to the oat mix before soaking it in the fridge overnight.

nutrition per serve Energy 1321 kJ (315 Cal); Fat 4.3 g; Carbohydrate 56.3 g; Protein 10 g

mixed berry couscous

This light breakfast is packed with fresh summer fruit and zesty spices. It's rich in carbohydrate, potassium and vitamin C as well as calcium in the yoghurt.

175 g (6 oz/1 cup) instant couscous

500 ml (17 fl oz/2 cups) unsweetened apple and blackcurrant juice

1 cinnamon stick

250 g (9 oz/2 cups) raspberries

250 g (9 oz/1⅔ cups) blueberries

250 g (9 oz/1⅔ cups) strawberries, hulled and halved

2 tsp lime or lemon zest, plus extra, to serve

1 tbs finely shredded mint

200 g (7 oz) low-fat plain or fruit-flavoured yoghurt

2 tbs maple syrup

Prep time: 10 minutes + standing + refrigeration time

Cooking time: 5 minutes

Serves 4

Place the couscous in a bowl. Pour the apple and blackcurrant juice into a small saucepan and add the cinnamon stick. Bring to the boil, then remove from the heat and pour over the couscous. Cover with plastic wrap and leave to stand for 5 minutes, or until the liquid has been absorbed. Remove the cinnamon stick. Refrigerate.

Separate the couscous grains with a fork, add the berries, lime zest and mint, and gently fold through. Spoon the mixture into 4 bowls. Top with a large dollop of plain or fruit-flavoured yoghurt and drizzle with the maple syrup. Serve chilled.

HINT: There are many other great flavours, including orange juice and dried fruits or fresh mango, peach, pear and apple.

nutrition per serve Energy 1520 kJ (362 Cal); Fat 0.8 g; Carbohydrate 73 g; Protein 11.2 g

fruit compote

A delicious snack or meal, this low-fat, slightly spicy fruit combo is an excellent source of fibre, potassium and the antioxidant, beta-carotene.

75 g (2¾ oz) dried apricots, quartered

75 g (2¾ oz) dried peaches or mango, quartered

75 g (2¾ oz) dried cherries or cranberries

50 g (1¾ oz) stoned dried dates, cut in half

25 g (1 oz) raisins or currants

250 ml (9 fl oz/1 cup) apple juice or water

1 small cinnamon stick

½ vanilla pod, split

2 pieces stem ginger, finely chopped

Prep time: 15 minutes
Cooking time: 10 minutes
Serves 4

Place the dried fruits in a saucepan and add the apple juice or water, cinnamon stick and vanilla pod. Bring to the boil, cover and simmer gently for 10 minutes.

Add the ginger off the heat and leave to cool. Transfer the compote to a covered bowl or airtight container and refrigerate, where it will last for at least a week. Serve a large spoonful on top of some yoghurt or good-quality muesli for a nourishing breakfast.

HINT: You can buy organic dried fruit or pre-soak the fruit in warm water or fruit juice and rinse to remove traces of the sulphites and mineral oils that are used to preserve them. Serve as suggested, or on its own with yoghurt for a wheat- and gluten-free diet.

nutrition per serve Energy 871 kJ (207 Cal); Fat 0.2 g; Carbohydrate 47.6 g; Protein 2.3 g

energy porridge
with stewed rhubarb

The mix of grains and rhubarb makes this breakfast more nutritious than regular porridge. It provides carbohydrate, fibre, B-group vitamins and potassium.

DRY PORRIDGE MIX
(makes 8 cups/16 serves)

600 g (1 lb 4 oz/6 cups) rolled oats

55 g (2 oz/½ cup) rolled rice flakes

60 g (2¼ oz/½ cup) rolled barley

60 g (2¼ oz/½ cup) rolled rye

30 g (1 oz/¼ cup) millet flakes

STEWED RHUBARB

350 g (12 oz) rhubarb, trimmed and washed

100 g (3½ oz/½ cup) soft brown sugar

¼ tsp ground mixed spice

Prep time: 5 minutes

Cooking time: 15 minutes

Serves 4

Place all the porridge ingredients in a large bowl and mix together well. The dry mix makes about 8 cups or enough for 16 serves. Store in a large airtight container for up to 2 months.

To make enough porridge for 4 serves, place 2 cups porridge mixture in a saucepan with 1.25 litres (44 fl oz/5 cups) water. Bring to the boil, then reduce the heat and simmer, stirring frequently, over a medium heat for 15 minutes, or until the porridge is thick. If it is too thick, add a little skim milk or water.

Meanwhile, to make the stewed rhubarb, chop the rhubarb into 2 cm (¾ in) lengths. Place in a saucepan with the sugar, mixed spice and 250 ml (9 fl oz/1 cup) water. Slowly bring to the boil, stirring to dissolve the sugar, then reduce the heat and simmer for 10 minutes, stirring often. Serve hot or cold with the energy porridge.

HINTS: The cooking time of the porridge will decrease considerably if you use quick-cooking oats (one-minute oats). Check the labels on the packets before purchase. However, quick-cooking oats have a higher GI value than slower-cooking oats (see page 11 for information on the glycaemic index).

If you have trouble finding some of these ingredients in your local supermarket, look for them at a good health-food shop.

nutrition per serve Energy 1238 kJ (295 Cal); Fat 3.6 g; Carbohydrate 57.8 g; Protein 6.2 g

ciabatta breakfast toasts

These crunchy toasts are great for breakfast or as a snack. The mix of plant foods and bacon provides a range of vitamins and minerals plus antioxidants and protein.

4 Roma (plum) tomatoes, halved

2 large field mushrooms, halved

oil spray

8 slices low-fat bacon (we used 97% fat-free)

160 g (5¾ oz/⅔ cup) low-fat cottage cheese

2 tbs chopped flat-leaf (Italian) parsley

1 tbs snipped chives

8 slices ciabatta bread, cut thickly at an angle and toasted

balsamic vinegar, to drizzle

Prep time: 15 minutes
Cooking time: 10 minutes
Serves 4

Preheat the grill (broiler). Place the tomatoes, cut-side-up, and the mushrooms on a large baking tray. Lightly spray with the oil. Season well with black pepper. Pat the bacon dry with paper towels and place on the tray. Grill the tomatoes, mushrooms and bacon for 5–8 minutes, or until cooked. Turn the bacon slices once and remove them as they cook and become crisp.

Combine the cottage cheese, parsley and chives. Spread thickly over the toasted bread. Arrange the tomatoes, mushrooms and bacon over the top. Drizzle (or spray) with a little balsamic vinegar.

HINT: Ciabatta is an oval-shaped, dense, crusty Italian bread. It is available from delicatessens. If you can't find it, you can use sourdough or another type of bread.

nutrition per serve Energy 1090 kJ (259 Cal); Fat 3.5 g; Carbohydrate 36.6 g; Protein 20.3 g

mushrooms with scrambled eggs & wholegrain bread

This is a classic breakfast, and filling as well! It provides good amounts of top-quality protein, vitamin A, iron and folate.

4 field mushrooms

spray oil

4 Roma (plum)
tomatoes, halved

3 tbs balsamic vinegar

4 eggs, lightly beaten

4 egg whites, lightly beaten

3 tbs low-fat milk

2 tbs snipped fresh chives

8 thick slices
wholegrain bread

Prep time: 10 minutes
Cooking time: 15 minutes
Serves 4

Trim the mushroom stalks to 2 cm (¾ in) above the cap. Wipe the mushrooms with paper towels to remove any dirt and grit.

Spray both sides of the mushrooms with the oil and place on a non-stick baking tray with the tomatoes. Drizzle the mushrooms and tomatoes with the balsamic vinegar, then sprinkle with salt and freshly ground black pepper and place under a medium grill (broiler) for 10–15 minutes, or until tender.

Meanwhile, place the eggs, egg whites, milk and chives in a bowl and whisk together to combine. Pour the mixture into a non-stick frying pan and cook over a low heat for 2–3 minutes, or until the egg begins to set, then gently stir with a wooden spoon to scramble.

Toast the wholegrain bread until golden brown, then cut on the diagonal. Serve with the mushrooms, tomato and scrambled egg.

HINT: Use omega-3 enriched eggs instead of regular eggs to get more of the essential omega-3 fatty acids. Omega-3 enriched eggs are available in most large supermarkets and some health-food shops.

nutrition per serve Energy 1362 kJ (324 Cal);
Fat 8.2 g; Carbohydrate 39.5 g; Protein 19.9 g

bagels with spinach, cottage cheese & baked beans

This nourishing meal has a wonderful mix of flavours and provides complete protein and good amounts of folate, niacin, beta-carotene and fibre.

425 g (15 oz) tin baked beans

200 g (7 oz) baby English spinach leaves

4 bagels, halved

250 g (9 oz/1 cup) low-fat cottage cheese

2 tomatoes, sliced, to serve

Prep time: 10 minutes
Cooking time: 10 minutes
Serves 4

Place the baked beans in a small saucepan and cook over a medium heat for 3 minutes, or until warmed.

Place the washed spinach in a medium saucepan, cover and cook over a medium heat for 2 minutes, or until wilted.

Toast the bagel halves and top with the cottage cheese and spinach. Spoon the baked beans over the top, and season with ground black pepper. Serve with the tomato slices for extra antioxidants and flavour.

HINTS: Many large supermarkets stock different types of bagels, including pumpernickel, wholemeal (wholewheat) and poppyseed varieties.

If you include baked beans and other legumes in your diet on a regular basis, they will be less likely to give you wind.

nutrition per serve Energy 1658 kJ (395 Cal); Fat 2.7 g; Carbohydrate 61.2 g; Protein 26.2 g

herb omelette, tomatoes & muffins

This full-flavoured dish is easy to prepare and is a good source of protein, vitamin A, antioxidants, folate and other B-group vitamins, and many minerals.

250 g (9 oz) yellow or red cherry tomatoes, halved

4 eggs, lightly beaten

4 tbs chopped mixed herbs (parsley, chives, oregano)

2 egg whites

oil spray

30 g (1 oz/¼ cup) grated low-fat Cheddar

1 handful baby rocket (arugula) leaves

4 wholemeal (wholewheat) or wholegrain English muffins, halved and toasted

Prep time: 15 minutes

Cooking time: 20 minutes

Serves 2

Preheat the oven to 180°C (350°F/Gas 4). Line a baking tray with baking paper. Place the tomatoes, cut-side-up, on the prepared tray. Season well with sea salt and ground black pepper. Bake for 15 minutes, or until softened. Reserve about one-third of the tomatoes for garnish.

Whisk together the eggs and mixed herbs in a bowl. Beat the egg whites in a small bowl with electric beaters until soft peaks form. Gently whisk the egg whites into the egg and herb mixture.

Preheat a grill (broiler). Heat an omelette pan or small frying pan with a 22 cm (8½ in) diameter (across the base) and lightly spray with the oil. Pour in half of the egg mixture and leave for 1–2 minutes, or until lightly browned underneath.

Scatter over half the cheese and place the pan under the grill for 1 minute, or until the egg is set and the cheese is melted. Top with half of the remaining tomatoes and half of the rocket. Fold the omelette in half and carefully slide from the pan onto a plate. Scatter over half of the reserved tomatoes.

Gently re-whisk the remaining egg mixture, then cook a second omelette in the same way as the first. Serve with the muffins.

HINTS: Use baby spinach instead of baby rocket, if preferred.

Use eggs enriched with omega-3 essential fatty acids to get more good fats in your diet. These are available in most supermarkets.

nutrition per serve Energy 2090 kJ (498 Cal); Fat 15.1 g; Carbohydrate 49.8 g; Protein 36.2 g

summer orange juice

This refreshing blend of citrus and stone-fruit juices is a rich source of folate, potassium and the antioxidants, beta-carotene and vitamin C.

3 oranges, peeled
5 small plums, stones removed
4 peaches, stones removed
10 apricots, stones removed

Juice the oranges, plums, peaches and apricots in a juice extractor or blender. Stir to combine.

Prep time: 10 minutes
Cooking time: Nil
Serves 2

nutrition per serve Energy 1388 kJ (331 Cal); Fat 1.1 g; Carbohydrate 62.2 g; Protein 7 g

maple banana breakfast

Here's the perfect booster drink, with calcium, phosphorus, vitamins and minerals.

350 ml (12 fl oz/1½ cups) low-fat milk
150 g (5½ oz/⅔ cup) low-fat vanilla yoghurt
2 very ripe bananas, chopped
1 large yellow peach, chopped
1 tbs wheat germ
2 tbs maple syrup

Blend the milk, yoghurt, banana, peach, wheat germ and maple syrup in a blender until smooth.

HINT: You can use low-fat soy milk in this recipe. If you use soy milk, make sure you choose one that has added calcium.

Prep time: 10 minutes
Cooking time: Nil
Serves 2

nutrition per serve Energy 1406 kJ (703 Cal); Fat 1.2 g; Carbohydrate 64.9 g; Protein 14.3 g

carrot, apricot & nectarine juice

One vegetable and two fruits combine to make this delicious and nutritious drink.

1 kg (2 lb 4 oz) baby carrots

10 apricots, stones removed

4 large nectarines, stones removed

ice cubes, to serve

lemon slices, to serve

Prep time: 10 minutes

Cooking time: Nil

Serves 2

Juice the carrots, apricots and nectarines in a juice extractor or use a blender. Stir to combine and serve over ice with lemon slices.

nutrition per serve Energy 1871 kJ (446 Cal); Fat 1.5 g; Carbohydrate 81 g; Protein 10.5 g

plum & prune tang

A refreshing drink providing calcium, phosphorus, potassium and some antioxidants.

200 g (7 oz/½ cup) plums, stoned and chopped

150 g (5½ oz/1 cup) prunes, pitted and chopped

250 g (9 oz/1 cup) low-fat vanilla yoghurt

125 ml (4 fl oz/½ cup) buttermilk

310 ml (10½ fl oz/1¼ cups) skim or calcium-enriched milk

8 large ice cubes

Prep time: 10 minutes

Cooking time: Nil

Serves 4

Blend the plums, prunes, yoghurt, buttermilk, milk and ice cubes in a blender until smooth.

nutrition per serve Energy 805 kJ (192 Cal); Fat 1.1 g; Carbohydrate 33.7 g; Protein 9.3 g

banana & honey smoothie

A hot favourite, this banana and honey combo is a good option for a light breakfast or snack. It contains carbohydrate, potassium and phosphorus.

2 ripe bananas
500 ml (17 fl oz/2 cups) low-fat soy milk
1 tbs honey or maple syrup
2 tbs low-fat plain yoghurt

Place the bananas and soy milk in a blender. Add the honey or maple syrup and yoghurt and blend until frothy.

HINT: You can substitute a variety of soft fresh fruits or rehydrated dried fruits for the bananas.

Prep time: 10 minutes
Cooking time: Nil
Serves 2

nutrition per serve Energy 1069 kJ (255 Cal); Fat 1.5 g; Carbohydrate 47.4 g; Protein 12.1 g

vegetable patch

This is a great way to get the goodness of different-coloured vegetables if you don't eat a variety of them on a regular basis. This drink packs a nutritious punch with folate, potassium, vitamin C and beta-carotene.

1 beetroot, scrubbed
10–12 carrots
2 green apples, stalks removed
2 large English spinach leaves
2 sticks celery

Juice the beetroot, carrots, apples, spinach and celery in a juice extractor or blender. Stir to combine and serve chilled.

Prep time: 10 minutes
Cooking time: Nil
Serves 2

nutrition per serve Energy 864 kJ (206 Cal); Fat 0.6 g; Carbohydrate 39.6 g; Protein 4.4 g

If you want to get the most out of your body, then you need to snack on nutritious foods (most of the time). Fatty take-away foods are generally low in vitamins, carbohydrate and minerals, and can decrease your alertness and performance if eaten before exercise. Use low-fat ingredients to make healthier versions of your favourite snacks. Low-fat, light meals are very useful for topping up your fuel stores before events.

snacks & light meals

mushroom pâté
with tortilla crisps

With far less fat than potato chips and regular pâté, this snack is a good option when you're looking for something savoury and crunchy to nibble on. It provides small to moderate amounts of the major vitamins as well as minerals.

1 tsp olive oil

1 small onion, chopped

2 cloves garlic, crushed

300 g (10½ oz) flat mushrooms, wiped clean and chopped

4 tbs white wine or water

80 g (2¾ oz /1 cup) fresh wholemeal (wholewheat) breadcrumbs

2 tbs thyme, plus extra to serve

2 tbs chopped flat-leaf (Italian) parsley

1 tbs lemon juice

4 large tortilla wraps, about 20 cm (8 in) in diameter, each cut into 8 wedges

oil spray

lemon pepper

sea salt

Prep time: 15 minutes + 1 hour refrigeration
Cooking time: 20 minutes
Serves 4–6

Heat the oil in a large, deep frying pan. Add the onion and garlic and cook, stirring, for 2 minutes without browning. Add the mushrooms and wine. Cook, stirring for 1 minute, then cover and simmer for 5 minutes, stirring once or twice. Remove the lid and increase the heat to evaporate any liquid. Cool.

Place the mushroom mixture, breadcrumbs, herbs and lemon juice in a food processor. Process until smooth and season well with salt and black pepper. Spoon into a serving bowl. Cover and refrigerate for at least 1 hour to allow the flavours to develop.

Preheat the oven to 180°C (350°F/Gas 4). Place the tortilla wedges on a large baking tray and lightly spray with the oil. Lightly sprinkle with the lemon pepper and sea salt. Bake for 8 minutes, or until crisp. Serve the pâté with the tortilla crisps.

HINTS: Three slices of wholemeal bread, crusts removed, will yield about 1 cup of crumbs.

Leftover tortilla crisps can be stored in the freezer for up to 1 month. Re-crisp them in a 170°C (325°F/Gas 3) oven for 5 minutes.

Lemon pepper is available in the spice department of supermarkets.

Be sparing with the amount of salt you use—it can exacerbate dehydration.

nutrition per serve (6) Energy 480 kJ (114 Cal); Fat 2.2 g; Carbohydrate 15.9 g; Protein 4.7 g

white bean & chickpea dip

This dip contains low-GI carbohydrate and is a delicious and easy way to eat beans and chickpeas. It provides many minerals, plus fibre and folate.

425 g (15 oz) tin cannellini (white) beans, rinsed and drained

425 g (15 oz) tin chickpeas, rinsed and drained

1½ tsp ground cumin

3 cloves garlic, crushed

2 tbs chopped flat-leaf (Italian) parsley

3 tbs lemon juice

1 tsp lemon zest

1 tbs tahini

Prep time: 10 minutes
Cooking time: Nil
Serves 3–4

Place all ingredients in a food processor and process for 30 seconds. With the motor still running, slowly add 3 tablespoons hot water to the processor in a thin stream until the mixture is smooth and 'dippable'. Serve at room temperature with crudités and pitta crisps.

HINT: Tahini is a thick paste made of ground sesame seeds. It is available at large supermarkets and health-food shops.

nutrition per serve (4) Energy 703 kJ (167 Cal); Fat 4.8 g; Carbohydrate 17.7 g; Protein 10.2 g

tamari nut mix

This snack is high in fat and kilojoules, but the fat is mostly monounsaturated. The nuts and seeds provide good amounts of a range of minerals, but make sure you eat this snack in moderation due to its high kilojoule content.

250 g (9 oz/1¾ cups) mixed raw unsalted nuts (almonds, Brazil nuts, peanuts, walnuts)

125 g (4½ oz/¾ cup) pepitas (pumpkin seeds)

125 g (4½ oz/1 cup) sunflower seeds

125 g (4½ oz/¾ cup) raw unsalted cashews

125 g (4½ oz/1 cup) raw unsalted macadamia nuts

125 ml (4 fl oz/½ cup) tamari

Prep time: 10 minutes + 10 minutes standing

Cooking time: 25 minutes

Serves 12

Preheat the oven to 140°C (275°F/Gas 1). You will need 2 large baking trays to bake the nuts.

Place the mixed nuts, pepitas, sunflower seeds, cashew nuts and macadamia nuts in a large bowl. Pour the tamari over the nuts and seeds, and toss together well, coating them evenly. Leave to stand for 10 minutes.

Spread the nut and seed mixture evenly over the baking trays and bake for 20–25 minutes, or until dry-roasted as desired. Cool completely. Makes 750 g (1 lb 10 oz/4 cups).

HINTS: Pepitas are peeled pumpkin seeds—they are available at most supermarkets and health-food stores.

Tamari is a fermented soy product similar to soy sauce. However, as it is made with 100 per cent whole soy beans it is much stronger than regular soy sauce, so you don't need to use as much. Tamari is also traditionally wheat-free.

Don't worry if the nut mixture does not seem crisp when you take it out of the oven. It won't crisp to its full potential until it is cooled.

Store in an airtight container away from direct sunlight for up to 2 weeks. Once stored, the nut mixture may become soft. If it does, lay the nuts on a baking tray and bake in a 150°C (300°F/Gas 2) oven for 5–10 minutes.

nutrition per serve Energy 1627 kJ (387 Cal); Fat 34.4 g (69% unsaturated fat); Carbohydrate 6 g; Protein 12.7 g

puffed corn mix

This snack is a great energy booster. It's best eaten at least 30 minutes before or after exercise as the fruit may upset your tummy if you're on the go.

170 g (6 oz/12 cups) packet puffed corn breakfast cereal

400 g (14 oz) packet dried fruit and raw nut mix

90 g (3¼ oz/1¼ cups) unprocessed natural bran

55 g (2 oz/1 cup) flaked coconut, toasted

60 g (2¼ oz/⅓ cup) pepitas (pumpkin seeds)

250 g (9 oz/¾ cup) honey

Prep time: 10 minutes
Cooking time: 20 minutes
Serves 20

Preheat the oven to 180°C (350°F/Gas 4). Line 4 baking trays with baking paper. Place the puffed corn, dried fruit and nut mix, bran, coconut and pepitas in a large bowl and mix together well.

Heat the honey in a saucepan over a low heat for 3 minutes, or until it thins to a pouring consistency. Pour over the puffed corn mixture and stir until all the dry ingredients are well coated with the honey.

Spread the mixture on the lined baking trays in a single layer and bake for 15 minutes, or until golden, turning the cereal several times during cooking. Cool completely before storing in an airtight container in a cool, dark place.

HINT: If you want to lower the fat content, leave out the flaked coconut.

nutrition per serve Energy 851 kJ (203 Cal); Fat 7.8 g; Carbohydrate 28.5 g; Protein 4 g

rye with tuna & mayonnaise

For good health, it's important to eat three to four portions of omega-3-rich fish each week. This recipe is a simple and delicious way to include fish in your diet.

210 g (7½ oz) tin tuna in brine or spring water, drained

90 g (3¼ oz/⅓ cup) low-fat mayonnaise

2 spring onions (scallions), finely chopped

1 coral lettuce, washed and drained

8 large slices rye bread

4 gherkins, thinly sliced

Prep time: 15 minutes
Cooking time: Nil
Serves 4

Place the tuna in a small bowl with the mayonnaise and spring onions and mix to combine.

Divide the lettuce leaves among 4 slices of bread. Top with the tuna and mayonnaise mixture. Divide the gherkins over the sandwich bases. Season to taste with salt and freshly ground black pepper. Top with the remaining 4 slices of bread.

nutrition per serve Energy 1359 kJ (324 Cal); Fat 6.2 g; Carbohydrate 46.8 g; Protein 17 g

sourdough with ham & cheese

An old favourite filling with a new twist — sourdough bread. This tasty sandwich includes ingredients from four food groups and provides a healthy dose of B-group vitamins, potassium, phosphorus and calcium.

4 tbs ready-made tomato chutney

2 tbs low-fat plain yoghurt

8 large slices sourdough bread

8 slices low-fat Cheddar

200 g (7 oz) shaved low-fat ham (we used 97% fat-free)

1 Lebanese (short) cucumber, shredded with a potato peeler

3 large handfuls snowpea (mangetout) sprouts

Prep time: 15 minutes

Cooking time: Nil

Serves 4

Combine the tomato chutney with the yoghurt. Spread the mixture on 4 slices of bread.

Add 2 slices of cheese, some ham, cucumber and a handful of sprouts. Top each slice with a bread lid.

nutrition per serve Energy 1480 kJ (352 Cal); Fat 8 g; Carbohydrate 42.1 g; Protein 28.6 g

lentil, corn & salad wraps

Full of goodness and easy to pack, wraps are snacks that you can eat at any time. This one is rich in carbohydrate, antioxidants, fibre, folate and potassium.

400 g (14 oz) tin brown lentils, rinsed and drained

425 g (15 oz) tin corn kernels, rinsed and drained

3 ripe tomatoes, seeded and finely chopped

1 small red onion, finely chopped

½ red capsicum (pepper), seeded and finely chopped

½ green capsicum (pepper), seeded and finely chopped

3 handfuls flat-leaf (Italian) parsley, chopped

2 tbs low-fat mayonnaise dressing (we used 99% fat-free)

8 lavash breads

125 g (4½ oz/½ cup) reduced-fat smooth ricotta

2 handfuls baby rocket (arugula) or baby English spinach leaves

Prep time: 15 minutes

Cooking time: Nil

Serves 4

Put the lentils in a large bowl and mash with a fork. Mix in the corn, vegetables and parsley. Stir through the mayonnaise.

Spread the breads with the ricotta, then divide the lentil salad and rocket or baby spinach leaves among the breads. Fold up the breads to enclose the filling. Wrap in baking paper or plastic wrap to secure.

nutrition per serve Energy 2213 kJ (527 Cal); Fat 7 g; Carbohydrate 86.4 g; Protein 21.7 g

salmon sandwiches

In terms of nutrients you can't beat this little beauty — omega-3 essential fatty acids, zinc, carbohydrate, calcium, phosphorus and B-group vitamins.

210 g (7½ oz) tin salmon in brine or spring water, drained

2 spring onions (scallions), finely chopped

2 small sticks celery, finely chopped

2 small spiced gherkins, finely chopped

2 tbs finely chopped parsley

2 tbs low-fat mayonnaise dressing (we used 97% fat-free)

2 tsp lemon juice

8 slices wholegrain bread

Prep time: 10 minutes

Cooking time: Nil

Serves 4

Place the salmon in a bowl, remove any skin and mash roughly with a fork. Add the spring onions, celery, gherkins and parsley. Stir through the mayonnaise and lemon juice. Season with salt and black pepper.

Spread 4 slices of the bread with the salmon mixture and place the remaining 4 slices of bread on top.

Stack the sandwiches together and firmly wrap in plastic wrap. Refrigerate until required, then cut into halves to serve.

nutrition per serve Energy 1095 kJ (261 Cal); Fat 6.8 g; Carbohydrate 33.3 g; Protein 14.8 g

soy sesame chicken legs

These portable snacks are a healthier alternative to take-away fried chicken legs, but still need to be eaten in moderation.

MARINADE
2 tbs honey
2 tbs sweet chilli sauce
2 tbs tomato sauce
2 tbs dark soy sauce
2 tbs light soy sauce

1.5 kg (3 lb 5 oz) skinless chicken drumsticks
2 tbs sesame seeds

Prep time: 15 minutes + marinating time
Cooking time: 45 minutes
Serves 4

Combine the marinade ingredients in a large non-metallic dish. Make 2–3 slits across each drumstick with a knife to allow the marinade to penetrate. Coat the drumsticks in the marinade, cover and refrigerate for at least 2 hours, or overnight. Turn in the marinade 2–3 times.

Preheat the oven to 180°C (350°F/Gas 4). Line a large baking tray with baking paper. Sprinkle the sesame seeds over the chicken. Bake for 45 minutes, or until cooked and golden, turning and coating with the marinade 2–3 times. Serve either warm or cold with bread and a mixed salad.

nutrition per serve Energy 1656 kJ (394 Cal); Fat 16.1 g; Carbohydrate 16.9 g; Protein 45.5 g

mushroom & spinach frittata

Frittatas are a filling snack and tasty to boot! This one's a good source of vitamin A and also provides vitamin D, calcium, folate and B-group vitamins.

oil spray

I red onion, thinly sliced

50 g (1¾ oz) low-fat bacon
(we used 97% fat-free),
thinly sliced

3 cloves garlic, crushed

90 g (3¼ oz) mushrooms,
thinly sliced

2 zucchini (courgettes), diced

I handful baby English
spinach leaves

4 eggs

60 ml (2 fl oz/¼ cup) skim or
no-fat milk

60 g (2¼ oz/½ cup) grated
low-fat Cheddar (we used
35% fat-reduced)

2 tbs shredded Parmesan

2 tbs basil, thinly shredded

Prep time: 20 minutes

Cooking time: 25 minutes +
cooling time

Serves 4

Spray a large, non-stick frying pan with oil. Heat the oil, add the onion, bacon and garlic and stir-fry for 4 minutes, or until soft. Add the mushrooms and zucchini and stir-fry for 3 minutes, or until the mushrooms are cooked and any liquid has evaporated. Stir in the spinach and cook until just wilted. Cool.

Whisk together the eggs and milk in a large bowl, stir in the cheeses, basil and cooled vegetable mixture.

Take a non-stick frying pan with a diameter of 18–20 cm/7–8 in (across the base) and spray with oil. Pour in the mixture and smooth the surface. Cook over a low heat for 10–13 minutes, or until mostly set. Take care not to burn the base.

Preheat a grill (broiler) to medium. Place the pan under the grill and cook for 3–5 minutes, or until firm and lightly browned on top. Serve warm or cold, cut into slices. Serve with bread and a salad.

nutrition per serve Energy 754 kJ (180 Cal); Fat 9.9 g; Carbohydrate 4.1 g; Protein 17.9 g

baked potatoes with herbed cottage cheese

Despite common myths, potatoes are not fattening — it's the things you eat with them that are the culprits. This recipe combines dry-baked potatoes with a low-fat, antioxidant-rich topping. Now, enjoy your meal without the guilt.

4 large potatoes

200 g (7 oz/½ bunch) English spinach, washed and chopped

250 g (9 oz/1 cup) low-fat cottage cheese

2 tbs chopped, mixed herbs (basil, parsley, oregano)

80 g (2¾ oz/½ cup) sun-dried capsicums (peppers), rinsed, drained and chopped

125 g (4½ oz) diced button mushrooms

Prep time: 15 minutes
Cooking time: 40 minutes
Serves 4

Preheat the oven to 200°C (400°F/Gas 6). Prick the potatoes a few times with a skewer. Place the potatoes on the oven rack and cook for 40 minutes, or until cooked through.

Place the spinach leaves, cottage cheese, herbs, sun-dried capsicums and mushrooms in a large bowl, and mix together well.

Cut a deep cross on the top of each potato. Divide the topping among the 4 baked potatoes. Serve while hot.

HINT: Dehydrated sun-dried capsicums are available from most supermarkets. To reconstitute, soak in warm water for 20 minutes, then drain. Otherwise, buy the ones prepared in oil and rinse well before using.

nutrition per serve Energy 920 kJ (219 Cal); Fat 2.3 g; Carbohydrate 27.7 g; Protein 17.1 g

turkish bread with cottage cheese & marinated tomatoes

This recipe is easy to make and scrumptious to eat. The bread is low in fat and rich in carbohydrate and the filling contains antioxidants and calcium.

4 Roma (plum) tomatoes, cut into thick slices

2 tbs balsamic vinegar

60 g (2¼ oz/1 cup) shredded basil

1 tsp sugar

1 loaf Turkish pide bread, cut into 4 slices, then sliced horizontally

250 g (9 oz/1 cup) low-fat cottage cheese

baby rocket (arugula) leaves, to serve

Prep time: 15 minutes
Cooking time: 5 minutes
Serves 4

Preheat the grill (broiler) to medium. Place the tomatoes in a non-metallic bowl with the balsamic vinegar, basil and sugar. Toss well to combine.

Toast the slices of bread under the grill until lightly toasted. Spread 4 slices with the cottage cheese.

Divide the tomato and basil mixture evenly over the cottage cheese, season with salt and freshly ground black pepper and top with rocket leaves. Top each slice with a bread lid.

nutrition per serve Energy 1415 kJ (337 Cal); Fat 5.7 g; Carbohydrate 50.5 g; Protein 19.8 g

ham, corn & polenta muffins

If you're looking to take some snacks with you to training or events, these savoury muffins are just the thing. They provide carbohydrate, some B-group vitamins and minerals and contain less fat than many commercial muffins.

110 g (3¾ oz/¾ cup) polenta

1 tbs sugar

210 g (7¼ oz/1⅔ cups) plain (all-purpose) flour

1 tbs baking powder

2 tbs oil

1 egg, lightly beaten

310 ml (11 fl oz/1¼ cups) skim milk

125 g (4½ oz) tin creamed corn

4 spring onions (scallions), thinly sliced

150 g (5½ oz) low-fat shaved ham (we used 97% fat-free), chopped

50 g (1¾ oz) low-fat Cheddar, grated (we used 93% fat-free)

Prep time: 15 minutes + 5 minutes cooling

Cooking time: 20 minutes

Makes 12

Preheat the oven to 200°C (400°F/Gas 6). Sift the polenta, sugar, flour and baking powder into a bowl. Place the oil, egg and skim milk in a separate bowl, mix together well and pour into the dry ingredients.

Add the creamed corn, spring onions, ham and cheese, and stir together with a large metal spoon until just combined. Do not overmix. The mixture should still be lumpy. Spoon the mixture into twelve 125 ml (4 fl oz/½ cup) non-stick muffin holes and bake for 20 minutes, or until risen and golden brown. Leave in the tin to cool for 5 minutes before turning out onto a wire rack to cool fully. Store in an airtight container.

HINT: Polenta is available at most supermarkets and health-food shops.

nutrition per muffin Energy 733 kJ (174 Cal); Fat 4.8 g; Carbohydrate 24.2 g; Protein 7.8 g

giant salmon balls

You'll be bowled over with these tasty salmon balls because they are oven-baked and not deep-fried. Team them with a salad and make a meal of them. They contain carbohydrate, protein, vitamins, minerals and omega-3 fatty acids.

3 potatoes, cut into 5 cm (2 in) pieces

100 g (3½ oz/½ cup) long-grain rice

50 g (1¾ oz/½ cup) raw rolled oats

415 g (14½ oz) tin red salmon in brine or spring water, drained and flaked

1 egg, lightly beaten

3 spring onions (scallions), chopped

2 tbs lemon juice

2 tbs sweet chilli sauce

80 g (2¾ oz/1 cup) fresh breadcrumbs

2 eggs, lightly beaten

200 g (7 oz/2 cups) dry breadcrumbs

oil spray

lemon wedges, to serve

Prep time: 35 minutes + 30 minutes refrigeration
Cooking time: 50 minutes
Makes 8 balls

Boil, steam or microwave the potatoes until tender. Drain, mash and set aside to cool. Cook the rice in a saucepan of boiling water for 10 minutes, or until tender. Drain and cool.

Place the potato, rice, oats, salmon, egg, spring onions, lemon juice, chilli sauce and fresh breadcrumbs in a bowl, and mix together well. Season with salt and pepper.

Divide the mixture into 8 portions and shape into balls. Dip in the egg, then in the dry breadcrumbs. Place on a baking tray lined with baking paper, cover and refrigerate for 30 minutes.

Preheat the oven to 200°C (400°F/Gas 6). Spray the salmon balls lightly with the oil and bake for 30 minutes, or until crisp, golden and heated through. Serve with lemon wedges and a large mixed salad.

nutrition per ball Energy 1434 kJ (341 Cal); Fat 8.7 g; Carbohydrate 45.4 g; Protein 18.1 g

baked sweet potato
& lentil rissoles

Big on flavour and low in fat, these slightly spicy rissoles are rich in carbohydrate and provide good amounts of beta-carotene, folate and niacin.

400 g (14 oz) tin brown lentils, rinsed and well drained

1 small onion, finely chopped

1 small green capsicum (pepper), finely chopped

1 carrot, grated

2 tbs finely chopped flat-leaf (Italian) parsley

425 g (15 oz/1⅓ cups) cooked and mashed sweet potato

140 g (5 oz/2 cups) fresh wholegrain breadcrumbs

1 tsp ground cumin

dry breadcrumbs, for coating

oil spray

SAUCE

185 ml (6 fl oz/¾ cup) tomato sauce

1–2 tsp curry powder

2 tsp lemon juice

Prep time: 20 minutes + refrigeration time

Cooking time: 40 minutes

Serves 4

Combine the lentils, onion, capsicum, carrot and parsley in a large bowl. Use clean hands to combine and mix in the sweet potato, breadcrumbs and cumin. Season well with salt and black pepper. Divide the mixture into 8 even-sized patties and refrigerate for at least 30 minutes to firm and develop flavour.

Preheat the oven to 200°C (400°F/Gas 6). Line a baking tray with a sheet of baking paper.

Coat the rissoles in the dry breadcrumbs. Spray the rissoles with the oil. Place on the prepared tray and bake, turning once or twice, for 35 minutes, or until crisp and golden.

Meanwhile, combine the sauce in a small saucepan and bring just to the boil. Set aside. Serve the rissoles hot or cold with the sauce, a mixed salad and wholegrain bread if you need extra carbohydrate.

HINTS: You can freeze leftover rissoles. Reheat the defrosted rissoles in the microwave. If you are short of time, you can pan-fry them. Heat a heavy-based, non-stick frying pan and spray with oil. Spray the rissoles with the oil. Cook for 2–3 minutes on each side, or until crisp and golden.

You will need 2–3 slices wholegrain bread to yield 2 cups breadcrumbs.

About 425 g (15 oz) sweet potato that has been peeled, chopped and steamed or boiled, then cooled and mashed will yield 1⅓ cups of cooked, mashed sweet potato.

nutrition per serve Energy 1292 kJ (308 Cal); Fat 2.9 g; Carbohydrate 55.6 g; Protein 11.1 g

layered cobs

Colour and flavour are the order of the day with these yummy cobs. They're the ideal snack to take to sporting events or on long hikes as they contain loads of carbohydrate energy. They also contain vitamins and minerals.

1 red capsicum (pepper)

oil spray

1 large zucchini (courgette), thinly sliced on the diagonal

2 slender eggplants (aubergines), thinly sliced on the diagonal

2 handfuls English spinach leaves

100 g (4½ oz/⅓ cup) ricotta

6 round bread rolls

1 tbs olive oil

1 clove garlic, crushed

1 tbs snipped chives

90 g (3¼ oz) low-fat leg ham (we used 97% fat-free), sliced into large pieces

Prep time: 45 minutes + overnight refrigeration

Cooking time: 30 minutes

Makes 6

Cut the capsicum into large pieces, removing the seeds and membrane. Cook, skin-side-up, under a hot grill (broiler) until blackened and blistered. Place in a plastic bag, allow to cool, then remove the skin. Cut the flesh into strips.

Lightly spray a non-stick frying pan with the oil, add the zucchini and eggplant in batches, and cook until golden and tender. Steam the washed spinach until just wilted. Cool slightly, squeeze out any liquid and roughly chop. Combine the ricotta and spinach, and season.

Cut the tops from the rolls and remove the bread inside, leaving a 1 cm (½ in) border on the inside of the shell. Combine the oil, garlic and chives, and brush inside each roll. Add a layer of capsicum and zucchini, spread with the ricotta and spinach mixture, then top with the ham and eggplant. Lightly press down, then replace the lids.

Cover the rolls with plastic wrap and place tightly in a baking dish. Place a tray on top and weigh down with heavy tins or weights. Refrigerate overnight.

Preheat the oven to 220°C (425°F/Gas 7). Remove the plastic wrap from the rolls. Place the rolls on a baking tray and bake for 10–15 minutes, or until crisp. Alternatively, skip this step and eat the cobs just as they are.

nutrition per serve Energy 1253 kJ (298 Cal); Fat 8.5 g; Carbohydrate 41.1 g; Protein 12.3 g

chicken & chilli baked potatoes

Everyone loves a baked potato, even more so if it has a low-fat — and delicious —
filling like this one. Depending on how hungry you are, this dish is ideal as a
light meal or a filling snack and provides antioxidants, fibre and potassium.

4 large potatoes

1 skinless chicken breast

125 g (4½ oz/½ cup) low-fat
plain yoghurt

1 tbs sweet chilli sauce

1 tbs chopped coriander
(cilantro) leaves

coriander (cilantro) sprigs,
to serve

Prep time: 15 minutes
Cooking time: 45 minutes
Serves 4

Preheat the oven to 200°C (400°F/Gas 6). Prick the potatoes a few
times with a skewer. Bake on the oven rack in the hot oven for
40 minutes, or until cooked through.

Meanwhile, bring a small saucepan of water to the boil, then reduce
the heat and simmer. Add the chicken breast and cook for 5 minutes.
Remove the pan from the heat, cover and leave to stand for
10 minutes to continue cooking the chicken. Leave the chicken
breast to cool, then finely shred.

Place the yoghurt, chilli sauce and coriander in a bowl and mix
together well. Scoop out some of the flesh of the potatoes, place
the yoghurt mixture in the potato shell and top with the shredded
chicken. Season to taste with salt and freshly ground black pepper.
Serve while hot, garnished with a sprig of fresh coriander.

*HINT: You can use half a barbecued chicken, if you prefer. Remove the
skin and bones, then finely shred.*

nutrition per serve Energy 937 kJ (223 Cal); Fat 3.7 g;
Carbohydrate 27.8 g; Protein 16.6 g

baked sweet potatoes mexicana

Like some spice? This dish is the perfect hot potato! It contains carbohydrate, fibre and antioxidants. Top with low-fat sour cream or yoghurt for extra calcium.

4 x 200 g (7 oz) orange sweet potatoes

oil spray

1 clove garlic, crushed

1 onion, finely chopped

250 g (9 oz) lean minced (ground) beef

300 g (10½ oz) tin red kidney beans, rinsed and drained

1 tbs tomato paste (purée)

325 g (11½ oz) jar mild tomato salsa

light sour cream, to serve

Prep time: 20 minutes

Cooking time: 40 minutes

Serves 4

Preheat the oven to 200°C (400°F/Gas 6). Prick the sweet potatoes a few times with a skewer. Bake on the oven rack for 40 minutes or until cooked through.

Meanwhile, heat a non-stick frying pan to medium. Lightly spray with the oil. Add the garlic and onion and cook for 2–3 minutes, or until softened. Add the beef and cook, breaking up any lumps with a wooden spoon, for 5 minutes, or until browned. Drain off any excess fat. Stir in the kidney beans, tomato paste and salsa. Bring to the boil, then reduce the heat and simmer for 10 minutes, or until slightly thickened.

Make a deep cut along the top of each cooked sweet potato. Divide the mixture among them and top with a dollop of light sour cream, if you like.

nutrition per serve Energy 1391 kJ (331 Cal); Fat 10.2 g; Carbohydrate 35.1 g; Protein 20.9 g

baked sweet potatoes
with avocado & corn salsa

A satisfying snack or light meal, this colourful dish packs a punch with nutrients such as monounsaturated fat and antioxidants, as well as fibre.

4 x 200 g (7 oz) orange sweet potatoes

I red onion, finely chopped

I avocado, finely chopped

I tbs lemon juice

130 g (4½ oz) tin corn kernels, drained

½ red capsicum (pepper), finely chopped

I tbs sweet chilli sauce

light sour cream or low-fat plain yoghurt, to serve

Prep time: 15 minutes

Cooking time: 40 minutes

Serves 4

Preheat the oven to 200°C (400°F/Gas 6). Prick the sweet potatoes a few times with a skewer. Bake on the oven rack for 40 minutes, or until cooked through.

Meanwhile, place the onion, avocado, lemon juice, corn and capsicum in a bowl and mix together well. Stir in the chilli sauce and season to taste with salt and freshly ground black pepper.

Make a deep cut along the top of each cooked sweet potato. Divide the topping among the sweet potatoes and add a dollop of light sour cream or low-fat plain yoghurt, if you prefer.

nutrition per serve Energy 1340 kJ (319 Cal); Fat 11.6 g; Carbohydrate 43.6 g; Protein 7 g

grilled ham, spinach
& tomato sandwiches

The traditional ham sandwich gets an exotic makeover using basil and Turkish pide bread. It makes a substantial snack or light meal and delivers a good dose of carbohydrate, protein, niacin and antioxidants.

I loaf Turkish pide bread

100 g (3½ oz/⅓ cup) low-fat cottage cheese

2 tbs finely shredded basil

2 tbs Dijon mustard

200 g (7 oz) shaved low-fat ham (we used 97% fat-free)

I handful baby English spinach leaves

2 large ripe tomatoes, sliced

oil spray

Prep time: 15 minutes
Cooking time: 15 minutes
Serves 4

Cut the bread into 4 pieces, then cut each piece in half, horizontally.

Place the cottage cheese and basil in a small bowl, and mix together.

Spread each piece of bread lightly with the mustard, then top with the cottage cheese mixture, ham, spinach and tomato.

Spray a sandwich grill (broiler) or toasted sandwich maker with oil, then cook each sandwich for 3 minutes, or until crisp and golden.

variation: Use thinly sliced turkey and cranberry sauce in place of the ham and mustard.

nutrition per serve Energy 1611 kJ (384 Cal); Fat 7.8 g; Carbohydrate 52.9 g; Protein 24.4 g

cream cheese & salmon bagels

Bagels are a great alternative to bread rolls and they come in a delicious range of flavours. Choose pumpernickel or grainy bagels to make this dish more filling. Nutrients in this recipe include omega-3 fatty acids, vitamins and minerals.

4 bagels, cut in halves

4 tbs low-fat cream cheese

I baby cos (romaine) lettuce

200 g (7 oz) smoked salmon

I red onion, thinly sliced

4 handfuls alfalfa sprouts

24 capers

few dill sprigs

juice of ½ lemon

Prep time: 15 minutes

Cooking time: 5 minutes

Serves 4

Preheat a grill (broiler) to medium. Cook the bagels under the grill until toasted.

Spread each half of the bagel with 1 tablespoon of the cream cheese. Divide the lettuce among the 4 bases. Top each bagel base with some of the smoked salmon, a few onion rings, alfalfa sprouts, some capers and a few sprigs of fresh dill. Sprinkle with a little lemon juice. Top with the bagel lid.

HINT: You can use low-fat ricotta cheese instead of the cream cheese for a lower-fat option.

nutrition per serve Energy 1603 kJ (382 Cal); Fat 8.4 g; Carbohydrate 50 g; Protein 24.8 g

rice paper rolls with prawns

A spicy favourite that's low in fat and packed with a wide variety of vitamins and minerals. What more could you ask for in a snack?

20 large cooked prawns (shrimp), peeled and deveined

1 small carrot

1 Lebanese (short) cucumber

125 g (4½ oz/1¾ cups) finely shredded red cabbage

8 spring onions (scallions)

1 handful mint, torn

2 handfuls coriander (cilantro) leaves

20 x 16 cm (8 x 6 in) square rice paper wrappers

DRESSING

125 ml (4 fl oz/½ cup) lime juice

2 tbs sweet chilli sauce

3 cloves garlic, crushed

1 long red chilli, seeded, finely chopped

1½ tbs grated palm sugar or soft brown sugar

1 tbs rice vinegar

1 tbs fish sauce

2 tbs chopped coriander (cilantro) leaves and stems

Prep time: 20 minutes
Cooking time: Nil
Makes 20 (4 serves)

Cut the prawns into 1 cm (½ in) slices, on the diagonal. Julienne the carrot into 4 cm (1½ in) lengths. Cut the cucumber into 1 cm (½ in) lengths. Thinly slice the spring onions on the diagonal. Put the prawns, cabbage, carrot, cucumber, spring onions, mint and coriander in a large bowl and toss to combine.

To make the dressing, put all the dressing ingredients in a small bowl and mix until well combined. Pour 125 ml (4 fl oz/½ cup) of the dressing over the prawn mixture and toss to combine. Working with one wrapper at a time, dip into a bowl of hot water for 10 seconds, or until softened, drain, then lay out on a flat surface.

Place 60 g (2 oz/¼ cup) of the mixture on one side of the wrapper, leaving a border at the sides. Fold in the sides and roll up tightly. Cover with a damp cloth and repeat with the remaining filling and wrappers to make 20 rolls. Serve with the remaining dressing as a dipping sauce.

nutrition per serve Energy 1354 kJ (322 Cal); Fat 1.8 g; Carbohydrate 49.5 g; Protein 24.9 g

prawn tortillas with mango salsa

These tortillas are quick and easy to make and are great as a snack or light meal. The salsa is an excellent source of two major antioxidants, beta-carotene and vitamin C. The prawns provide many minerals.

MANGO SALSA

½ red onion, finely chopped

2 mangoes, peeled and finely chopped

4 vine-ripened tomatoes, seeded and finely chopped

1 Lebanese (short) cucumber, peeled, seeded and finely chopped

1 stick celery, thinly sliced

3 handfuls mint, chopped

2 tbs ready-made fat-free French dressing

8 x 20 cm (8 in) flour tortilla wraps

16 raw prawns (shrimp), peeled and deveined, tails intact

oil spray

coriander (cilantro) leaves, to serve

lemon wedges, to serve

Prep time: 20 minutes
Cooking time: 10 minutes
Serves 4

Preheat a barbecue flat plate or oven to 180°C (350°F/Gas 4). Combine the mango salsa ingredients in a large bowl.

Wrap the tortillas in foil and place on a warm part of the barbecue, or in the oven for 8 minutes.

Lightly spray the flat plate or frying pan with the oil. Add the prawns and cook, turning occasionally, for 2–3 minutes, or until just cooked through. Spray the prawns with a little of the oil as they cook.

To serve, fold the tortillas into 4. Arrange the tortillas, salsa and prawns on serving plates and garnish with the coriander leaves and lemon wedges.

HINTS: If fresh mango is not available you can use tinned mango or diced fresh peaches, nectarines or pawpaw.

You can use any fat-free salad dressing for this dish.

nutrition per serve Energy 1296 kJ (309 Cal) Fat 2.8 g; Carbohydrate 47.5 g; Protein 18.7 g

beef pittas with pineapple salsa

A more nutritious substitute for take-away pizzas or Mexican food, this quick meal provides protein, iron and zinc, and good doses of carbohydrate and antioxidants.

1 tsp olive oil

1 onion, finely chopped

1 stick celery, finely chopped

½ red capsicum (pepper), seeded and finely chopped

400 g (14 oz) lean minced (ground) beef

1 tsp ground cumin

½ tsp ground coriander

1 tbs tomato paste (purée)

250 g (9 oz/1 cup) pasta sauce

240 g (8¾ oz) tin red kidney beans, rinsed and drained

4 large wholemeal (wholewheat) pitta breads

250 g (9 oz/1 cup) low-fat plain yoghurt

PINEAPPLE SALSA

½ pineapple

4 vine-ripened tomatoes

310 g (10½ oz) tin corn kernels, rinsed and drained

50 g (1¾ oz/½ bunch) coriander (cilantro) leaves, chopped

1 tbs lemon juice

Prep time: 15 minutes

Cooking time: 20 minutes

Serves 4

Heat the oil in a large, non-stick frying pan. Add the onion, celery and capsicum and cook, stirring, for 2 minutes, or until softened. Increase the heat, add the meat and cook, stirring, for 5 minutes, or until the meat changes colour. Break up any lumps with a fork.

Stir in the spices and tomato paste. Add the pasta sauce and 125 ml (4 fl oz/½ cup) water. Simmer and stir frequently for 8 minutes, or until cooked and slightly reduced. Stir in the kidney beans.

To make the pineapple salsa, peel and finely chop the pineapple. Seed and finely chop the tomatoes. Combine the salsa ingredients, reserving half of the coriander leaves for garnish.

Meanwhile, preheat the oven to 180°C (350°F/Gas 4). Wrap the pitta breads in foil and heat for 5 minutes, or until heated through.

To serve, top each pitta with the meat filling and top with the yoghurt. Sprinkle with the reserved coriander and serve with the salsa.

nutrition per serve Energy 2672 kJ (636 Cal); Fat 11.6 g; Carbohydrate 82.6 g; Protein 40.8 g

pitta pizzas

Always feel guilty when eating pizza? You can have your pizza and eat it too with these low-fat varieties. And just look at the range of delicious toppings!

4 large wholemeal (wholewheat) pitta pocket breads

130 g (4¾ oz/½ cup) ready-made tomato salsa

½ red onion, thinly sliced

90 g (3¼ oz) mushrooms, thinly sliced

60 g (2¼ oz) low-fat ham (we used 97% fat-free), thinly sliced

90 g (3¼ oz/½ cup) black olives in brine, rinsed, drained, pitted and chopped

1 tbs capers, rinsed, drained and chopped

80 g (2¾ oz/½ cup) low-fat fetta

10 g (¼ oz/¼ cup) sprigs rosemary

100 g (3½ oz/1 cup) grated low-fat mozzarella (we used 35% reduced-fat)

Prep time: 15 minutes
Cooking time: 20 minutes
Serves 4

Preheat the oven to 200°C (400°F/Gas 6). Place the pitta breads on a large baking tray or on two smaller trays. Spread each with the salsa. Scatter over the onion, mushrooms, ham, olives and capers.

Crumble over the fetta and top with the rosemary sprigs and mozzarella. Bake for 20 minutes. Serve immediately.

variations: Use tomato pasta sauce or salsa sauce on the base, then choose from the following toppings: low-fat ham, pineapple pieces, sliced capsicum (pepper), onion or olives marinated in brine.

For a meaty topping, try leftover savoury mince or spaghetti bolognaise and low-fat Cheddar. For a little spice, try salami, corn kernels, sliced green capsicum, onion, tomato and low-fat fetta.

A tasty vegetarian option is artichoke hearts, tomato and zucchini (courgette) slices, ricotta and low-fat fetta.

And an easy seafood version uses tuna in spring water, sliced mushroom and capsicum and low-fat Cheddar.

nutrition per serve Energy 1506 kJ (358 Cal); Fat 9.6 g; Carbohydrate 41.9 g; Protein 22.9 g

Soups and salads can be part
of a meal or a meal in
themselves, and are an easy
way to add a variety of
vegetables and legumes to
your diet. Soups can be made
ahead of time and individual
portions can be frozen, so
you have healthy meals that
can be quickly reheated when
you're too tired to cook.
Nutritious salads can also
be made quickly if you have
a well-stocked pantry and
fridge. Most ingredients are
available all year round.

soups & salads

prawn, scallop & noodle soup

Healthy, hearty and flavoursome, this seafood soup contains low-GI soba noodles and has nutritious minerals such as potassium and iodine.

4 dried shiitake mushrooms

100 g (3½ oz) dried soba (buckwheat) or somen noodles

1 x 10 g (¼ oz) sachet bonito-flavoured soup stock

80 g (2¾ oz) carrots, cut into thin batons

150 g (5½ oz) firm tofu, cut into cubes

16 raw prawns (shrimp), peeled and deveined, tails intact

8 scallops

2 spring onions (scallions), finely chopped

1 tbs mirin

shichimi togarashi (Japanese seven-spice seasoning mix), optional

Prep time: 10 minutes + 15 minutes soaking

Cooking time: 20 minutes

Serves 4

Put the mushrooms in a bowl and cover with 300 ml (10½ fl oz) of boiling water. Place a saucer on top of the mushrooms to submerge them in the liquid, and leave to soak for 15 minutes.

Meanwhile, bring a saucepan of water to the boil for the noodles. Cook the noodles until just tender, then drain. Return the cooked noodles to the pan and cover to keep warm.

In a large saucepan, mix 1 litre (35 fl oz/4 cups) of water and the stock. Drain the mushrooms and add the mushroom-soaking liquid to the pan. Chop the mushroom caps, discarding the stalks.

Add the mushrooms and carrot to the pan and bring the liquid to the boil. Reduce the heat to a simmer and cook for 5 minutes. Add the tofu, prawns, scallops, spring onions and mirin to the pan. Cook at a gentle simmer for a further 3–4 minutes, or until the prawns have turned pink and are cooked through and the scallops are firm and opaque.

Meanwhile, pour hot water over the noodles and swish the noodles around in the water to separate and warm them. Divide the noodles between 4 large bowls and pour the hot soup over them, dividing the seafood equally. Serve immediately, offering the shichimi togarashi as a flavouring to sprinkle over the top.

HINTS: Although this recipe suggests soba or somen noodles you can use any type. If bonito stock sachets and shichimi togarashi are not available you can use a good-quality fish or chicken stock and omit the flavouring.

nutrition per serve Energy 1117 kJ (266 Cal); Fat 5.3 g; Carbohydrate 22.5 g; Protein 32.4

chicken corn chowder

Make a super-nutritous meal of this delicious chowder by serving it with crusty bread and salad. The soup contains potassium, beta-carotene and folate.

180 g (6¼ oz) skinless chicken breast fillet, trimmed

1 litre (35 fl oz/4 cups) chicken stock or water

1 large onion, diced

2 potatoes, diced

1 stick celery, diced

1 large carrot, grated

420 g (14½ oz) tin creamed corn

310 g (10¾ oz) tin corn kernels, drained

125 ml (4 fl oz/½ cup) skim or no-fat milk

3 tbs finely chopped flat-leaf (Italian) parsley

Prep time: 20 minutes
Cooking time: 35 minutes
Serves 4

Cut 2–3 slits across the thickest part of the chicken fillet. Heat the stock or water in a large, heavy-based saucepan. Poach the chicken fillet for 10 minutes, or until just cooked through. Remove the chicken from the pan and set aside. When cooled, use two forks to thinly shred the chicken flesh.

Add the onion, potatoes, celery and carrot to the saucepan. Bring to the boil, then lower the heat and simmer for 20 minutes, or until the potato is cooked.

Stir in the creamed corn, corn kernels, milk, chicken and parsley. Stir gently to heat through.

HINTS: Instead of poaching the chicken you can use the skinless fat-free breast meat from a barbecued chicken. Frozen precooked chicken breasts are also available in the freezer section of the supermarket.

You can freeze the soup into serving-sized portions. They will keep for up to 1 month.

This is a thick soup; however, you can add more stock or milk to make it thinner, if you prefer.

nutrition per serve Energy 1453 kJ (346 Cal);Fat 5.5 g; Carbohydrate 48.9 g; Protein 20.6 g

noodle soup with pork & vegetables

If you marinate the pork beforehand, this delicious soup doesn't take long to prepare. It provides B-group vitamins, potassium, phosphorus, iron and zinc.

1 tbs dark soy sauce

1 tbs rice wine

2 tsp soft brown sugar

400 g (14 oz) pork fillet (tail end), trimmed

1 tsp canola oil

1 litre (35 fl oz/4 cups) chicken stock

150 g (5½ oz) dried egg noodles

3 tbs light soy sauce

3 tbs rice wine

oil spray

1 stick celery, cut into thin 5 cm (2 in) batons

4 spring onions (scallions), cut into 5 cm (2 in) pieces

1 long red chilli, seeded and sliced

225 g (8 oz) tin sliced bamboo shoots, drained

2 handfuls baby English spinach leaves

Prep time: 20 minutes + marinating time
Cooking time: 25 minutes
Serves 4

Combine the dark soy sauce, rice wine and sugar in a shallow non-metallic dish. Pat the pork dry with paper towels. Coat the pork fillet in the soy marinade. Set aside for at least 15 minutes.

Heat the oil in a large wok. Add the meat, brown on all sides, then lower the heat and cook, turning occasionally, for 10 minutes, or until cooked through. Remove to a side dish and cover with foil.

Wipe out the wok with paper towels. Heat the stock in the wok and bring to the boil. Add the noodles and stir to break up. Add 250 ml (9 fl oz/1 cup) water, bring to the boil again and cook for 3 minutes. Strain the stock into a large saucepan and set aside the noodles. Add the light soy sauce and rice wine to the stock and set the saucepan over a low heat.

Wipe out the wok again with paper towels. Heat the wok and spray with the oil. Add the celery, spring onions and red chilli and stir-fry for 2 minutes. Add the bamboo shoots and spinach and stir-fry for 1 minute, or until heated through and the spinach has wilted.

Divide the noodles into 4 large, deep, serving bowls. Cut the pork into thin slices on the diagonal. Arrange the pork and vegetables in the bowls and pour over the hot broth—you may not need all the broth, but you should use about 250 ml (9 fl oz/1 cup) per serve.

HINT: You can buy rice wine in the Asian section of supermarkets and in Asian stores. Use dry sherry if it is not available.

nutrition per serve Energy 1652 kJ (393 Cal); Fat 7.4 g; Carbohydrate 39.6 g; Protein 35.3 g

hearty bean & vegetable soup

Vegie soups don't come any better than this. Full of goodness and wonderful flavours, this vitamin-rich dish hits the spot every time.

1 tsp olive oil

100 g (3½ oz) pancetta, trimmed and diced

1 leek, thinly sliced

2 cloves garlic, chopped

1 stick celery, thinly sliced

1 large carrot, diced

2 waxy potatoes, diced

2 litres (70 fl oz/8 cups) chicken stock

400 g (14 oz) tin chopped tomatoes

80 g (2¾ oz/½ cup) macaroni

155 g (5½ oz/1 cup) frozen peas, defrosted

1 zucchini (courgette), thinly sliced

185 g (6¼ oz) cauliflower, cut into small florets

400 g (14 oz) tin cannellini (white) beans, rinsed and drained

1 handful flat-leaf (Italian) parsley, chopped

grated Parmesan, to serve (optional)

Prep time: 25 minutes

Cooking time: 40 minutes

Serves 4–6

Heat the oil in a large saucepan. Add the pancetta, leek and garlic and cook, stirring, over a low heat for 10 minutes without browning. Add the celery, carrot and potatoes. Cook and stir for a further 5 minutes.

Pour in the stock and add the tomatoes. Bring slowly to the boil, then simmer for 15 minutes. Stir in the pasta, peas, zucchini, cauliflower and beans. Simmer for a further 10 minutes, or until the pasta is cooked. Stir in the parsley.

Serve with grated Parmesan, if desired, and crusty or wholegrain bread.

HINTS: You can use red kidney beans instead of cannellini beans, if you prefer.

If pancetta is not available you can use 97% fat-free bacon.

Freeze any leftover soup into serving-sized portions. It will keep for up to 1 month.

nutrition per serve (6) Energy 1174 kJ (279 Cal); Fat 7.6 g; Carbohydrate 31.1 g; Protein 17.7 g

italian lemon & spinach soup

Traditional Italian flavours abound in this soup. The lemon zest gives it a real boost. The soup contains beta-carotene, folate and potassium. And, if you serve it with bread, you'll get extra carbohydrate.

2 tsp olive oil

I onion, finely diced

½ leek, finely diced

2 sticks celery, finely diced

3 cloves garlic, thinly sliced

½ tsp grated lemon zest

1.5 litres (52 fl oz/6 cups) chicken stock

90 g (3¼ oz/I cup) small pasta

200 g (7 oz/½ bunch) English spinach leaves, shredded

4 tbs lemon juice

I handful basil, torn

Prep time: 20 minutes

Cooking time: 20 minutes

Serves 4

Heat the oil in a large, heavy-based saucepan over a medium heat. Add the onion, leek, celery, garlic and lemon zest and cook for 10 minutes, or until soft and translucent.

Add the chicken stock and bring to the boil. Add the pasta and simmer for 8 minutes, or until tender. Remove from the heat, add the spinach, lemon juice and basil, and season well with sea salt and black pepper to taste. Serve immediately with crusty Italian bread.

Hint: If you are a vegetarian, you can use vegetable stock in this recipe.

nutrition per serve Energy 1287 kJ (306 Cal); Fat 7.6 g; Carbohydrate 40.6 g; Protein 15.3 g

red lentil & parsnip soup

A meal in itself, this hearty soup can be stored in the fridge for four days and reheated to suit. It's a good source of fibre, niacin, potassium and beta-carotene.

1 tsp olive oil

1 onion, chopped

2 cloves garlic, crushed

1 parsnip, peeled and chopped

1 stick celery, chopped

1 large carrot, chopped

1 tsp ground cumin

1 tbs tomato paste (purée)

400 g (14 oz) tin chopped tomatoes

180 g (6¼ oz/1 cup) red lentils

1 litre (35 fl oz/4 cups) chicken or vegetable stock or water

1 tbs lemon juice

3 tbs chopped flat-leaf (Italian) parsley

Prep time: 20 minutes

Cooking time: 30 minutes

Serves 4

Heat the oil in a large, heavy-based saucepan. Add the onion and garlic and stir-fry for 2 minutes, or until softened. Add the parsnip, celery and carrot and cook, covered, on a low heat for 8 minutes to sweat the vegetables. Stir once or twice and take care not to brown.

Stir in the cumin, tomato paste, tomatoes, lentils and stock or water. Bring to the boil, then lower the heat and simmer for 20 minutes, or until the lentils are cooked. Season well with salt and pepper. Stir in the lemon juice and parsley. Serve with crusty bread and salad.

HINT: This is a thick soup; add more stock or water to make it thinner. You can also freeze the soup in serving-sized portions for up to 1 month.

nutrition per serve Energy 1287 kJ (306 Cal); Fat 5.5 g; Carbohydrate 39.2 g; Protein 20 g

chicken & sweet potato salad

Tender pieces of chicken are mixed with vegetables and herbs to make a meal that's rich in antioxidants, niacin, potassium and folate. Serve with grainy bread and low-fat cheese for extra carbohydrate, protein and calcium.

4 Roma (plum) tomatoes, quartered lengthways

300 g (10½ oz) eggplant (aubergine), quartered lengthways

oil spray

500 g (1 lb 2 oz) orange sweet potato, peeled and cut into 2 cm (¾ in) slices

1 large red onion, sliced into thin wedges

1 barbecued chicken

2 tbs chopped coriander (cilantro) leaves

2–3 tbs balsamic vinegar

2 handfuls rocket (arugula)

Prep time: 30 minutes
Cooking time: 30 minutes
Serves 6

Preheat the oven to 200°C (400°F/Gas 6). Place the tomatoes and eggplant on a large, non-stick baking tray, spray with a little oil and season with salt and freshly ground black pepper. Bake, turning the eggplant halfway through, for 25–30 minutes.

Meanwhile, steam the sweet potato for 15 minutes, or until just tender. Place in a large bowl with the tomato and eggplant.

Lightly spray a small non-stick frying pan with oil, add the onion and cook over a low heat for 6 minutes, or until golden. Set aside.

Remove the skin and bones from the chicken and discard. Cut the chicken meat into bite-sized pieces and add to the vegetables with the coriander and 1 tablespoon balsamic vinegar. Toss gently.

Place the rocket on a platter, then the chicken mixture and top with the onion. Drizzle with the remaining balsamic vinegar to taste. Serve with thick slices of wholegrain bread.

HINT: You can substitute the barbecued chicken with freshly cooked chicken breast fillets or you can use precooked chicken breast meat, which you'll find in the freezer section of the supermarket.

nutrition per serve Energy 1042 kJ (248 Cal); Fat 7.9 g; Carbohydrate 16 g; Protein 26.2 g

light chicken caesar salad

An old favourite with a trim, new look, this delicious Caesar salad is perfect for people on the go. It provides good amounts of vitamins, plus protein.

4 thick slices wholemeal (wholewheat) or wholegrain bread

oil spray

50 g (1¾ oz) low-fat bacon (we used 97% fat-free), thinly sliced

1 large cos (romaine) lettuce, outer leaves and core removed

2 cooked chicken breast fillets, cut into 3 cm (1¼ in) cubes

4 anchovy fillets in brine, drained, rinsed and halved lengthways

2 tbs finely chopped flat-leaf (Italian) parsley

35 g (1¼ oz/⅓ cup) shredded Parmesan

LOW-FAT DRESSING

125 g (4½ oz/½ cup) low-fat plain yoghurt

3 tbs low-fat mayonnaise dressing (we used 97% fat-free)

1 tbs Dijon mustard

1 tbs lemon juice

¼ tsp Worcestershire sauce

1–2 cloves garlic, crushed

Prep time: 20 minutes

Cooking time: 15 minutes

Serves 4

Preheat the oven to 180°C (350°F/Gas 4). Remove the crusts from the bread and cut into 2 cm (¾ in) cubes. Place on a tray. Bake for 12 minutes, or until lightly browned. Turn once to brown evenly. Set aside to cool and crisp.

Lightly spray a small frying pan with oil. Heat the pan, add the bacon and stir-fry for 2 minutes, or until cooked. Drain on paper towels.

Meanwhile combine the low-fat dressing ingredients in a bowl, adding the garlic to taste. Season with black pepper.

Break the lettuce leaves into smaller pieces in a large serving bowl. Add the chicken, bread, bacon, half of the anchovies, parsley and Parmesan. Toss through two-thirds of the dressing. Scatter over the remaining anchovies, parsley and Parmesan. Drizzle over the remaining dressing. Serve with crusty bread for extra carbohydrate.

HINTS: You can use poached or barbecued chicken breast in this recipe. Remove any skin and fat.

If you can only find anchovies in oil, soak them in milk for a few minutes, then pat dry to remove the oil.

nutrition per serve Energy 1294 kJ (308 Cal); Fat 11.1 g; Carbohydrate 16.7 g; Protein 34.4 g

tuna & bean salad

Healthy, filling and tasty, this salad provides protein, low-GI carbohydrate and fibre, making it a great choice for those watching their weight. It also contains antioxidants such as vitamin C, beta-carotene and flavonoids.

100 g (3½ oz) green beans, trimmed and chopped

400 g (14 oz) tin butter beans, rinsed and drained

425 g (15 oz) tin tuna in brine or spring water, drained

200 g (7 oz) cherry tomatoes, halved

1 red onion, thinly sliced

100 g (3½ oz) mixed salad leaves

100 g (3½ oz/1 small bunch) baby rocket (arugula)

DRESSING

2 tsp extra-virgin olive oil

3 tbs lemon juice

1 tsp honey

2 cloves garlic, crushed

2 tbs chopped fresh dill

Prep time: 20 minutes + 10 minutes refrigeration
Cooking time: 5 minutes
Serves 4

Steam the green beans until tender, then rinse under cold water and drain well. Place the green beans and butter beans, tuna, tomato and onion in a bowl and toss well.

To make the dressing, whisk all the ingredients together. Pour over the tuna mixture, cover and refrigerate for 10 minutes.

Combine the salad leaves and rocket, then arrange on a salad platter. Top with the tuna mixture and serve with slices of wholegrain bread.

HINT: You can use any variety of ready-made, fat-free salad dressing for this recipe, if you prefer.

nutrition per serve Energy 697 kJ (166 Cal); Fat 4.7 g; Carbohydrate 7.4 g; Protein 21.2 g

herbed pasta & salmon salad

This high-carb salad takes very little time to prepare and is great for topping up your fuel tanks. It contains some essential omega-3 fatty acids and good amounts of potassium, antioxidants, folate and phosphorus.

400 g (14 oz) small shell pasta

250 g (9 oz) cherry tomatoes, quartered, or halved, if small

1 large yellow capsicum (pepper), seeded and diced

2 sticks celery, thinly sliced

3 spring onions (scallions), thinly sliced

80 g (2¾ oz/½ cup) pitted green olives in brine, drained and chopped

2 tbs capers, rinsed and chopped (optional)

200 g (7 oz) smoked salmon, sliced

1 handful basil, finely shredded

3 tablespoons finely chopped flat-leaf (Italian) parsley

125 ml (4 fl oz/½ cup) ready-made fat-free Italian salad dressing

Prep time: 15 minutes
Cooking time: 10 minutes
Serves 4

Cook the pasta in a large saucepan of boiling water for 10 minutes, or until just cooked. Rinse under cold water to cool. Drain. Place in a large bowl.

Place all the other ingredients into the bowl with the pasta, add the dressing and toss together.

HINT: Any type of small pasta shapes and fat-free dressing can be used in this recipe.

nutrition per serve 2027 kJ (483 Cal); Fat 3.8 g; Carbohydrate 83.4 g; Protein 24.1 g

salmon salad with horseradish

Lots of goodness in this dish — and delicious too. There are antioxidants, fibre and easily absorbed iron and zinc. Serve with bread to add more carbohydrate.

500 g (1 lb 2 oz) kipfler potatoes, scrubbed

300 g (10½ oz/½ bunch) watercress, washed and sprigs removed

2 Lebanese (short) cucumbers, halved lengthways, sliced on diagonal

400 g (14 oz) smoked salmon, cut into 4 cm (1½ in) pieces

3 tbs horseradish cream

2 cloves garlic, crushed

4 tbs light sour cream

1 tsp coarsely grated lemon zest

3 tsp lemon juice

2 tsp chopped dill

Prep time: 15 minutes
Cooking time: 10 minutes
Serves 4

Bring a large saucepan of salted water to the boil and cook the potatoes for 8–10 minutes, or until tender, then drain well. Cut into 1.5 cm (¾ in) slices on the diagonal. Cool.

Place the potatoes, watercress, cucumbers and smoked salmon in a large bowl. Combine the horseradish, garlic, sour cream, lemon zest and juice and dill in a small bowl. Scoop over the salad and toss until well combined. Season with salt and pepper to taste. Serve immediately with crusty bread.

HINT: To reduce the fat content you can use plain low-fat yoghurt instead of sour cream.

nutrition per serve Energy 1337 kJ (318 Cal); Fat 11 g; Carbohydrate 21.7 g; Protein 29.7 g

cannellini bean & rocket salad

A zesty Mediterranean-style salad packed with folate, antioxidants and fibre.

3 red capsicums (peppers), halved and seeded

1 clove garlic, crushed

zest of 1 lemon

4 tbs coarsely chopped flat-leaf (Italian) parsley

400 g (14 oz) tin cannellini (white) or flageolet beans

2 tbs lemon juice

2 tbs extra-virgin olive oil

100 g (3½ oz/1 small bunch) rocket (arugula) or mixed salad leaves

Prep time: 20 minutes

Cooking time: 15 minutes

Serves 2 as a main course or 4 as a starter

Grill (broil) the capsicums until the skin has blackened, then place in a sealed plastic bag to cool. Remove the skin, then cut into strips. Combine the garlic with the lemon zest and parsley.

Combine the cannellini or flageolet beans with half of the parsley mixture, 1 tablespoon lemon juice, 1 tablespoon extra-virgin olive oil, and salt and pepper to taste. Place the rocket or salad leaves on a large plate and mix with the remaining lemon juice and extra-virgin olive oil.

Scatter the beans over the leaves, then lay the capsicum strips on top, along with the remaining parsley mixture. Season with salt and pepper and serve immediately as a starter, a light meal, or to accompany grilled (broiled) meat or fish.

HINT: Instead of tinned beans, you can soak 250 g (9 oz) dried beans overnight, then boil with a dash of oil and no salt for 30–40 minutes, or until tender.

nutrition per serve (4) Energy 726 kJ (173 Cal); Fat 9.6 g; Carbohydrate 12.5 g; Protein 7 g

minty beef noodle salad

A low-GI dish with a tangy flavour, this salad provides antioxidants, folate, iron and zinc. Suitable as a light meal or a quickly prepared dinner.

oil spray

500 g (1 lb 2 oz) piece lean beef rump steak

250 g (9 oz) dry thin rice vermicelli noodles

250 g (9 oz) cherry tomatoes, halved

2 x 100 g (3½ oz) packets baby Asian salad leaves

1 Lebanese (short) cucumber, peeled, seeded and thinly sliced

¼ red onion, cut into thin slivers

6 radishes, thinly sliced

1 handful mint

DRESSING

3 tbs lime juice

3 tbs light soy sauce

2 tbs fish sauce

2 tbs grated palm sugar or soft brown sugar

2 small red chillies, seeded and finely chopped

Prep time: 20 minutes
Cooking time: 10 minutes
Serves 4

Heat a large, non-stick frying pan. Spray with the oil. Pat the meat dry with paper towels. Season well with black pepper. Put the meat in the pan and brown on both sides. Cook for a further 5–8 minutes, or until cooked as desired. Cover with foil and set aside for 5 minutes, then cut into thin slices.

Combine the dressing ingredients in a small bowl, stirring to dissolve the sugar.

Cover the noodles with boiling water and set aside for 5 minutes, or until softened. Drain and cool. Use scissors to cut into smaller lengths.

Combine the cherry tomatoes, salad greens, cucumber, onion, radishes and mint leaves in a large bowl. Toss through the noodles and beef, then pour over the dressing. Serve immediately.

nutrition per serve Energy 1763 kJ (420 Cal); Fat 7.3 g; Carbohydrate 51.1 g; Protein 34.3 g

tuna niçoise

This classic salad has colour and flavour and is surprisingly filling. It's also low in fat and contains a good dose of major vitamins and minerals.

350 g (12 oz) small new potatoes

150 g (5½ oz) green beans, trimmed and halved

2 eggs

175 g (13 oz) mixed salad leaves

2 artichoke hearts in brine, rinsed, drained and quartered

4 ripe Roma (plum) tomatoes, cut into wedges

1 small red capsicum (pepper), seeded and sliced

425 g (15 oz) tin tuna in brine or spring water, drained and broken into chunks

125 ml (4 fl oz/½ cup) ready-made fat-free French dressing

50 g (1¾ oz/⅓ cup) pitted black olives in brine, rinsed and drained

1 tbs capers, rinsed and drained

2 tbs chopped flat-leaf (Italian) parsley

Prep time: 20 minutes
Cooking time: 15 minutes
Serves 4

Cook the potatoes in a saucepan of boiling water for 10 minutes, or until just cooked. Take care not to overcook. Drain and cool under cold water. Cut each in half.

Meanwhile, plunge the beans into a saucepan of boiling water for 2 minutes. Drain and cool under cold water. Place the eggs in a small saucepan of water. Bring to the boil, stirring to centre the yolks. Boil for 5–8 minutes, drain and cool under cold water. Peel and cut into quarters.

Arrange the salad leaves over the base of a large, shallow serving bowl. Top with the beans, eggs, artichokes, tomatoes, capsicum and tuna. Pour over the dressing and scatter over the olives, capers and the parsley. Serve with fresh or toasted Turkish pide bread for extra carbohydrate and B-group vitamins.

nutrition per serve Energy 1118 kJ (266 Cal); Fat 5.3 g; Carbohydrate 24.3 g; Protein 26.7 g

sardines with greek-style salad

A delicious way to eat sardines and reap the benefits of their excellent nutrient content. Eaten with their bones, sardines provide good amounts of calcium and phosphorus, which are further boosted by the fetta cheese.

6 Roma (plum) tomatoes, each cut into quarters

2 Lebanese cucumbers (short), peeled, halved, seeded and sliced

I fennel bulb, thinly sliced

I small red onion, thinly sliced

2 sticks celery, sliced

80 g (2¾ oz/½ cup) pitted Kalamata olives in brine, rinsed and drained

120 g (4¼ oz) reduced-fat fetta

4 tbs ready-made fat-free Greek dressing

2 x 105 g (3½ oz) tins sardines in spring water, drained

few small sprigs oregano (optional)

8 slices crusty bread

Prep time: 15 minutes

Cooking time: Nil

Serves 4

Put the tomatoes, cucumbers, fennel, onion, celery and olives in a large serving bowl. Crumble over the fetta, then toss through the dressing. Arrange the sardines over the top and scatter over the oregano sprigs, if you like. Serve with the hot crusty bread to top up your carbohydrate energy stores.

HINT: You can use any flavoured fat-free dressing such as Italian or French.

nutrition per serve Energy 1595 kJ (380 Cal); Fat 11.1 g; Carbohydrate 41.9 g; Protein 24.7 g

warm chicken & pasta salad

A nourishing meal with a variety of delicious flavours. It contains low-GI carbohydrate from the sweet potato, pasta and beans. It has vitamin K, iron and zinc, and is rich in antioxidants, folate, potassium and phosphorus.

750 g (1 lb 10 oz) orange sweet potato, cut into 2 cm (¾ in) cubes

250 g (9 oz) cherry tomatoes, halved

oil spray

2 x 200 g (7 oz) skinless chicken breast fillets

310 g (11 oz/2 bunches) slender asparagus, trimmed and cut into thirds

375 g (13 oz) macaroni

400 g (14 oz) tin cannellini (white) beans, rinsed and drained

3 handfuls baby rocket (arugula) leaves

3 tbs ready-made fat-free French dressing

Prep time: 20 minutes

Cooking time: 45 minutes

Serves 6

Preheat the oven to 200°C (400°F/Gas 6). Place the sweet potato at one end of a large, non-stick baking dish and the tomatoes at the other end, cut-side-down. Lightly spray with oil and bake for 45 minutes, turning halfway through. Remove the tomatoes after 30 minutes.

Meanwhile, lightly spray a chargrill plate or barbecue flat plate with oil and heat over a high heat. Cook the chicken for 5 minutes on each side, or until cooked through.

Bring a large saucepan of water to the boil, add the asparagus and cook for 1 minute. Remove with a slotted spoon and plunge into iced water. Drain. Return the water to the boil and cook the macaroni for 10 minutes, or until tender. Drain and keep warm.

Slice the chicken into 1 cm (½ in) thick strips and place in a large bowl with the roasted sweet potato and tomatoes, asparagus, pasta, beans and rocket and toss until combined. Add the dressing to the salad and toss until well combined. Season to taste and serve immediately.

HINT: You can use any short pasta in this recipe. Cook according to manufacturer's directions. Use other beans, if preferred, such as kidney, butter, soya or chickpeas.

nutrition per serve Energy 1946 kJ (463 Cal); Fat 5.3 g; Carbohydrate 70.2 g; Protein 29.2 g

beef & noodle salad

This nutritious salad is even more appealing with an aromatic lemon grass dressing. It is a good source of iron, zinc, niacin and folate.

DRESSING

2 tbs finely chopped lemon grass, tender inner part only

1 small red chilli

3 tbs light soy sauce

3 tbs lime juice

1 tbs fish sauce

1 tbs grated palm sugar or soft brown sugar

1 tsp grated ginger

500 g (1 lb 2 oz) lean sirloin steak

oil spray

200 g (7 oz) cellophane (bean thread) noodles

1 Lebanese (short) cucumber

1 small red onion

4 ripe Roma (plum) tomatoes

1 tbs thinly shredded ginger

90 g (3¼ oz/1 cup) bean sprouts

1 handful mint, torn

1 handful basil, torn

1 handful coriander (cilantro) leaves

Prep time: 15 minutes + marinating time

Cooking time: 10 minutes

Serves 4

Bruise the lemon grass using a mortar and pestle or a heavy object such as a rolling pin. Seed and finely chop the chilli. Combine the dressing ingredients using a mortar and pestle or in a bowl and stir to dissolve the sugar. Put 1 tablespoon of the dressing in a shallow non-metallic dish with the meat. Coat the meat with the dressing and marinate for at least 15 minutes. Set aside the remaining dressing.

Spray a non-stick frying pan or chargrill pan with oil. Heat the oil until very hot. Add the steak and cook for 2–3 minutes on each side, or until cooked as desired. Remove and set aside for 5 minutes, then slice thinly.

Place the noodles in a large bowl and cover with boiling water. Set aside for 4 minutes, drain well and refresh under cold water. Use scissors to cut into short lengths.

Cut the cucumbers in half, then thinly slice on the diagonal. Cut the onion into thin wedges. Cut the tomatoes into quarters.

Place the noodles, cucumber, onion, tomatoes, ginger, sprouts and herbs in a large bowl. Add the meat and reserved dressing. Toss together gently. Serve immediately.

nutrition per serve Energy 1704 kJ (406 Cal); Fat 8.5 g; Carbohydrate 51.5 g; Protein 29.2 g

thai chicken salad

Delicate Thai herbs and flavours dress up this chicken salad beautifully. It's packed with beta-carotene, niacin, potassium, phosphorus, iron and zinc.

100 g (3½ oz) dried rice vermicelli

250 g (9 oz) minced (ground) chicken

200 g (7 oz) tin water chestnuts, drained and chopped

2 tbs fish sauce

2 tbs lime juice

1 stem lemon grass, white part only, finely chopped

3 spring onions (scallions), finely chopped

3 tbs chopped fresh Thai basil

3 tbs chopped mint

Prep time: 15 minutes + 10 minutes soaking
Cooking time: 5 minutes
Serves 4

Soak the vermicelli in boiling water for 10 minutes, or until tender. Drain and pat dry.

Place the chicken, water chestnuts, fish sauce, lime juice, lemon grass and 3 tablespoons water in a frying pan, and stir over a medium heat for 5 minutes, or until cooked. Set aside to cool. Transfer to a bowl and add the spring onions, basil, mint and vermicelli. Toss well to combine. Serve immediately.

nutrition per serve Energy 834 kJ (198 Cal); Fat 5.8 g; Carbohydrate 20.5 g; Protein 14.9 g

roast mushroom & baby bean salad

This tasty salad teams well with meat, fish or cheese. It contains mostly monounsaturated fat, plus fibre, folate, antioxidants and potassium.

600 g (1 lb 4 oz) field mushrooms, brushed clean

2 tbs olive oil

3 cloves garlic, crushed

2 tbs lemon juice

6 French shallots, root ends trimmed, skin left on

1½ tbs tarragon vinegar

2 tsp finely chopped tarragon

1 tbs finely chopped flat-leaf (Italian) parsley

200 g (7 oz) baby green beans, trimmed

2 handfuls rocket (arugula)

Prep time: 15 minutes

Cooking time: 35 minutes

Serves 4

Preheat the oven to 200°C (400°F/Gas 6). Place the mushrooms in a single layer in a large roasting pan. Add the oil, garlic, lemon juice and shallots and gently toss until coated. Roast for 30 minutes, occasionally spooning over the juices. Remove from the oven and cool to room temperature. Slip the shallots from their skins and discard the skin.

Pour the cooking juices into a large mixing bowl. Add the tarragon vinegar, tarragon and parsley. Mix and season well.

Blanch the beans in boiling salted water for 2 minutes, or until just tender. Drain well and, while still hot, add to the dressing. Allow to cool to room temperature.

Cut the mushrooms into quarters, or eighths if large, and add to the beans with the shallots and rocket. Gently toss together and serve on 1 platter or 4 individual serving plates.

HINT: Tarragon vinegar is available at most supermarkets or delicatessens. Use a white wine vinegar if tarragon is not available.

nutrition per serve Energy 609 kJ (145 Cal); Fat 9 g; Carbohydrate 5.2 g; Protein 7.6 g

Pasta is a favourite food among athletes, because it is quick to prepare, rich in carbohydrate, and low in fat when served with low-fat sauces. Wholemeal pasta provides extra fibre and B-group vitamins, and can be more filling than white pasta, and thus is good for weight control. For pasta meals to be balanced, they should be served with a low-fat sauce that contains vegetables, legumes or lean meat, poultry or fish.

pasta

macaroni cheese with roast tomato salad

This reduced-fat version of macaroni cheese makes a tasty high-carb meal and is a good source of niacin, vitamin A, folate, phosphorus and calcium.

6 Roma (plum) tomatoes

2 tsp balsamic vinegar

2 tbs finely shredded basil

250 g (9 oz) macaroni

2 tsp low-fat butter

1 small onion, finely chopped

3 cloves garlic, crushed

2 tbs plain (all-purpose) flour

500 ml (17 fl oz/2 cups) evaporated skim milk (undiluted)

2 tsp Dijon mustard

100 g (3½ oz) grated reduced-fat Cheddar (we used 25% reduced-fat)

250 g (9 oz/1 cup) low-fat cottage cheese

2 tbs chopped flat-leaf (Italian) parsley

oil spray

20 g (¾ oz/¼ cup) fresh breadcrumbs

¼ tsp ground nutmeg

30 g (1 oz) grated Parmesan

Prep time: 25 minutes

Cooking time: 1½ hours

Serves 4

Preheat the oven to 180°C (350°F/Gas 4). Cut the tomatoes in half lengthways. Place on a rack over an oven tray, season well with salt and pepper, and cook for 1 hour, or until they have dried out slightly. Remove from the oven, drizzle with the balsamic vinegar and top with the shredded basil leaves. Place on a serving platter and set aside.

Meanwhile, cook the macaroni in a large saucepan of boiling salted water until just tender and drain. Melt the butter in a large saucepan over low heat. Add the onion and garlic and cook for 5 minutes, or until softened. Stir in the flour and cook over a low heat for 2 minutes. Remove from the heat and gradually whisk in the milk. Return to the heat and stir constantly until the sauce boils and thickens. Reduce the heat and simmer for 2 minutes. Remove from the heat, stir in the mustard, Cheddar, cottage cheese and parsley. Add the macaroni and mix gently.

Spray a 1.5 litre (52 fl oz/6 cup) ovenproof dish with olive oil. Spoon the mixture into the dish. Combine the breadcrumbs, nutmeg and Parmesan and sprinkle over the top. Bake for 25 minutes, or until golden and bubbling. Serve with the roast tomato salad, a mixed green salad and thick slices of wholegrain bread.

nutrition per serve Energy 2327 kJ (554 Cal); Fat 12.7 g; Carbohydrate 69.1 g; Protein 38.8 g

spinach shells in tomato sauce

This low-fat meal is suitable for vegetarians who eat dairy products and it provides good amounts of calcium, B-group vitamins and antioxidants.

30 (220 g/7 oz) large pasta shells

250 g (9 oz) frozen leaf spinach, defrosted

500 g (1 lb 2 oz/2 cups) low-fat cottage cheese

250 g (9 oz/1 cup) low-fat ricotta

2 spring onions (scallions), finely chopped

1 tsp nutmeg

500 ml (17 fl oz/2 cups) bottled puréed tomatoes

250 ml (9 fl oz/1 cup) vegetable stock or water

60 g (2¼ oz/½ cup) grated low-fat Cheddar (we used 50% reduced-fat)

Prep time: 20 minutes
Cooking time: 55 minutes
Serves 4–6

Cook the pasta in a large saucepan of boiling salted water for 10 minutes, or until just tender. Drain and cool under cold water.

Using clean hands, squeeze the excess moisture from the spinach. Place in a large bowl, add the cottage and ricotta cheeses, spring onions and nutmeg. Season well with salt and black pepper. Combine well using a fork.

Preheat the oven to 180°C (350°F/Gas 4). Combine half the puréed tomatoes and half the stock or water and pour over the base of a 32 x 25 x 5 cm (12½ x 10 x 2 in) ovenproof dish. Spoon the spinach mixture into the pasta shells and place them in a single layer over the sauce. Spread over the remaining combined puréed tomatoes and stock or water and sprinkle over the cheese.

Bake for 45 minutes, or until the pasta is cooked. Serve hot with a mixed green salad.

HINTS: This meal can be prepared in advance.

You may find bottled puréed tomatoes labelled as passato, which is an Italian term that commonly refers to puréed, sieved tomatoes. Alternatively, you can use a ready-made pasta sauce.

nutrition per serve (6) Energy 1427 kJ (340 Cal); Fat 7.7 g; Carbohydrate 36.9 g; Protein 28.4 g

seafood pasta

Lovers of seafood will put this tasty dish on the favourites list. It's easy to make and contains carbohydrate as well as iron, zinc and antioxidants.

12 black mussels, scrubbed clean and beards removed

125 ml (4 fl oz/½ cup) white wine

1 tsp olive oil

1 large onion, chopped

3 cloves garlic, finely chopped

2 x 400 g (14 oz) tins chopped tomatoes

2 tbs tomato paste (purée)

1 tsp dried oregano

500 g (1 lb 2 oz) bucatini or spaghetti

8 raw prawns (shrimp), peeled and deveined, tails intact

300 g (10½ oz) fresh or frozen seafood marinara mixture

1 large handful basil, shredded

Prep time: 25 minutes

Cooking time: 35 minutes

Serves 4

Discard any opened mussels. Place the mussels in a large saucepan with the wine and 125 ml (4 fl oz/½ cup) water. Cook, covered, for 3 minutes, or until the mussels have opened. Discard any unopened ones. Remove the mussels and reserve the liquid.

Heat the oil in a large saucepan, add the onion and garlic and cook for 2–3 minutes, or until softened. Add the tomatoes, tomato paste and oregano leaves. Stir in the reserved mussel cooking juice. Bring to the boil, then simmer for 20 minutes, or until reduced and thickened a little.

Meanwhile, cook the pasta in a large saucepan of boiling salted water for 10 minutes, or until just tender. Drain.

Add the prawns and marinara mixture to the sauce. Cook over a low heat for 3 minutes, or until the seafood is cooked. Toss the sauce, mussels and basil through the pasta. Serve immediately.

HINT: You can use any thick pasta, such as fettuccine or penne.

nutrition per serve Energy 2876 kJ (685 Cal); Fat 6.3 g; Carbohydrate 98.8 g; Protein 47.6 g

fettuccine with tuna & tomato

This carbohydrate-rich meal is great for topping up your fuel tanks. It is also an easy way to include fish in your diet. One serve of this dish provides you with plenty of antioxidants, niacin and potassium as well as some iron.

2 tsp olive oil

1 large onion, cut into thin wedges

2 cloves garlic, crushed

80 g (2¾ oz) button mushrooms, thinly sliced

2 x 400 g (14 oz) tins chopped tomatoes, roughly chopped

2 tsp sugar

1 tsp freshly ground black pepper

3 tbs capers, rinsed, drained and chopped

425 g (15 oz) tin tuna in brine or spring water, drained and flaked

1 large handful flat-leaf (Italian) parsley, finely chopped

1 handful basil, shredded

500 g (1 lb 2 oz) fettuccine

grated Parmesan, to serve (optional)

Prep time: 20 minutes

Cooking time: 20 minutes

Serves 4

Heat the olive oil in a large, deep, heavy-based saucepan. Add the onion and garlic and cook for 2 minutes, or until softened. Add the mushrooms, tomatoes, sugar, pepper and capers. Bring to the boil, then lower the heat and simmer for 15 minutes. Stir in the flaked fish, parsley and basil.

Meanwhile, cook the pasta in a large saucepan of boiling salted water for 10 minutes, or until just tender. Drain and return to the saucepan. Toss through the sauce. Divide into serving bowls and serve with the Parmesan cheese, if you prefer.

nutrition per serve Energy 2665 kJ (634 Cal); Fat 6.7 g; Carbohydrate 100.4 g; Protein 37.7 g

low-fat lasagne

No need to go without lasagne — just go low-fat. Serve with salad.

oil spray

1 large onion, finely chopped

3 large cloves garlic, crushed

1 stick celery, diced

1 carrot, diced

125 g (4½ oz) button mushrooms, thinly sliced

500 g (1 lb 2 oz) lean minced (ground) beef

1 tsp chopped dried oregano

250 ml (9 fl oz/1 cup) red wine

500 ml (17 fl oz/2 cups) beef stock

2 tbs tomato paste (purée)

2 x 400 g (14 oz) tins chopped tomatoes

500 g (1 lb 2 oz/1 bunch) English spinach, stalks removed

375 g (13 oz) lasagne sheets

WHITE SAUCE

20 g (¾ oz) reduced-fat butter

4 tbs plain (all-purpose) flour

375 ml (13 fl oz/1½ cups) skim milk

150 g (5½ oz/⅔ cup) ricotta

85 g (3 oz) low-fat Cheddar

Prep time: 25 minutes

Cooking time: 2¼ hours

Serves 6

Heat a large, non-stick saucepan and spray with the oil. Add the onion and cook for 2 minutes. Add the garlic, celery, carrot and mushrooms, and cook for a further 2 minutes. Add the mince and cook over a high heat for 5 minutes, or until cooked, breaking up any lumps with the back of a spoon. Add the oregano and wine and cook for 3–4 minutes, or until most of the liquid has evaporated.

Add the stock, tomato paste and tomatoes and season. Reduce the heat to low and simmer, covered, for 1½ hours, stirring occasionally to prevent it from catching on the bottom. If the sauce is too thin, remove the lid and simmer until reduced and thickened. Cool slightly. Wilt the washed spinach for 1 minute in a covered saucepan. Drain.

Meanwhile, to make the white sauce, melt the butter in a saucepan over a medium heat. Stir in the flour and cook for 1 minute. Remove from the heat and gradually stir in the milk. Return to the heat and stir constantly until the sauce boils and thickens. Reduce the heat and simmer for 2 minutes. Stir through the ricotta until smooth.

Arrange one-third of the pasta over the base of a 4 litre (140 fl oz/16 cup) rectangular ovenproof dish. Spoon over half the beef, then cover with half the spinach. Cover with another layer of pasta and spoon over the remaining beef. Cover with the remaining spinach, then the remaining pasta. Spread over the white sauce to cover. Grate the cheese over the top. Bake for 30 minutes, or until golden. Stand for 5 minutes before slicing.

HINT: Use pre-cooked lasagne sheets.

nutrition per serve Energy 2295 kJ (546 Cal); Fat 15.6 g; Carbohydrate 52.4 g; Protein 48.4 g

herrings in tomato sauce pasta

The zesty tomato sauce combines well with the pasta and herrings to make this a nutritious, low-GI meal. The olives contain monounsaturated fat and the fish provides omega-3 fat. The tomato sauce is a good source of antioxidants.

1 tsp olive oil

2 cloves garlic, chopped

1 small red chilli, seeded and chopped

2 x 400 g (14 oz) tins chopped tomatoes

125 g (4½ oz/¾ cup) black olives in brine, pitted and chopped

2 tbs capers, rinsed and drained

1 large handful basil, shredded

1 tsp sugar

200 g (7 oz) tin herring fillets in tomato sauce

500 g (1 lb 2 oz) spaghetti

shredded basil, extra, to serve

grated Parmesan, to serve

Prep time: 15 minutes

Cooking time: 25 minutes

Serves 4

Heat the oil in a heavy-based saucepan. Add the garlic and chilli and cook briefly for 1 minute without browning. Add the tomatoes, olives, capers, basil and sugar. Stir well and simmer, uncovered, for 20 minutes, or until thick and reduced. Stir through the fish to break up a little. Season with pepper to taste.

Meanwhile, cook the pasta in a large saucepan of boiling salted water for 10 minutes, or until just tender. Drain and return to the saucepan. Toss through the sauce. Divide between 4 plates, top with basil and Parmesan and, if you like, serve with a salad.

nutrition per serve Energy 2570 kJ (612 Cal); Fat 10.6 g; Carbohydrate 102.5 g; Protein 22.5 g

spaghetti bolognaise & salad

Who can resist this all-time favourite? Low fat and rich in carbohydrate, this dish is also a good source of niacin, antioxidants, potassium, iron and zinc.

I tsp olive or canola oil

I large onion, finely chopped

3 cloves garlic, crushed

I stick celery, diced

I carrot, diced

500 g (1 lb 2 oz) lean minced (ground) beef

I tbs chopped oregano

250 ml (9 fl oz/1 cup) red wine

500 ml (17 fl oz/2 cups) beef stock

2 tbs tomato paste (purée)

2 x 400 g (14 oz) tins chopped tomatoes

350 g (12 oz) spaghetti

SALAD

150 g (5½ oz) mixed lettuce leaves

I Lebanese (short) cucumber, sliced on diagonal

2 tbs ready-made fat-free French dressing

Prep time: 20 minutes

Cooking time: 2 hours

Serves 4

Heat the olive or canola oil in a large, non-stick saucepan over a medium heat. Add the onion and cook for 2–3 minutes, or until softened. Add the garlic, celery and carrot and cook for 2–3 minutes, or until softened. Add the meat and cook over a high heat for 5 minutes, or until cooked, breaking up any lumps with the back of a spoon. Add the oregano and wine and cook for 3–4 minutes, or until almost all the liquid has evaporated. Add the stock, tomato paste and tomatoes and season.

Reduce the heat to low and simmer, covered, for 1½ hours, stirring occasionally to prevent it from catching on the bottom. If the sauce is too thin, remove the lid and simmer until reduced and thickened.

Cook the pasta in a large saucepan of boiling salted water for 10 minutes, or until tender. Drain and toss through the bolognaise sauce. Serve with the salad.

Make the salad just before serving. Combine the lettuce and cucumber in a bowl and add the dressing. Season to taste and toss until well combined.

HINT: Use 1 teaspoon dried oregano leaves if fresh is not available.

nutrition per serve Energy 2643 kJ (629 Cal); Fat 12.9 g; Carbohydrate 74.9 g; Protein 26.9 g

spaghetti with chicken meatballs

This dish is great for active people who train in the afternoons or evenings—it's quick to prepare and has many of the nutrients needed to repair and refuel a tired body, including carbohydrate, protein, antioxidants, zinc and iron.

TOMATO SAUCE

1 tsp olive oil

2 cloves garlic, crushed

2 x 400 g (14 oz) tins crushed tomatoes

CHICKEN MEATBALLS

500 g (1 lb 2 oz) minced (ground) chicken

2 cloves garlic, crushed

20 g (¾ oz/¼ cup) fresh breadcrumbs

2 tbs chopped basil

¼ tsp cayenne pepper

oil spray

375 g (13 oz) spaghetti

2 tbs chopped basil

30 g (1 oz) Parmesan, grated

basil, extra, to serve

Prep time: 25 minutes

Cooking time: 30 minutes

Serves 4

To make the sauce, heat the oil in a large, non-stick pan over a medium heat. Add the garlic and cook for 1 minute, or until just turning golden. Add the tomatoes and season well with salt and freshly ground black pepper. Reduce the heat and simmer for 15 minutes, or until thickened and reduced.

Meanwhile, line an oven tray with baking paper or foil. Combine the chicken, garlic, breadcrumbs, basil and cayenne pepper in a large bowl and season well. Using damp hands, roll tablespoons of the mixture into balls and place on the prepared tray.

Heat a non-stick frying pan over a medium heat and spray well with the oil. Cook the meatballs in batches, turning, for 3–4 minutes, or until they are golden. Transfer the meatballs to the sauce and simmer for a further 10 minutes, or until they are cooked through. Add the basil and check the sauce for seasoning.

Meanwhile, cook the spaghetti in a large saucepan of boiling salted water for 10 minutes, or until tender. Drain well. Toss the spaghetti with the meatballs and sauce and serve with the grated Parmesan and the extra basil.

nutrition per serve Energy 2640 kJ (628 Cal); Fat 16.1 g; Carbohydrate 75.5 g; Protein 40.4 g

tomato & olive pasta

All the flavours of the Mediterranean are in this tasty vegetarian dish. It also contains good amounts of amino acids, antioxidants, folate and potassium.

750 g (1 lb 10 oz) vine-ripened tomatoes, finely chopped

1 small red onion, finely chopped

2 cloves garlic, finely chopped

110 g (4 oz/½ cup) chopped pitted green olives

3 tbs capers, rinsed and chopped

1 tsp dried oregano

1 tbs olive oil

1 tbs white wine vinegar

500 g (1 lb 2 oz) spaghetti

300 g (10½ oz) tin soya beans, rinsed and drained

1 handful oregano

Prep time: 15 minutes + 1 hour standing time
Cooking time: 10 minutes
Serves 4

Combine the tomatoes, onion, garlic, olives, capers and dried oregano in a bowl. Whisk together the oil and vinegar in a small bowl, then toss through the tomato mixture. Season with salt and pepper. Cover and set aside for at least 1 hour to allow the flavours to develop.

Meanwhile, cook the pasta in a large saucepan of boiling salted water for 10 minutes, or until just tender. Drain and return to the saucepan. Toss the tomato mixture and soya beans through the hot pasta. Garnish with the oregano leaves. Serve with a lettuce salad.

HINTS: For full flavour, use good-quality tomatoes.

To add calcium to this meal, use grated Parmesan cheese.

nutrition per serve Energy 2450 kJ (583 Cal); Fat 9.1 g; Carbohydrate 98.8 g; Protein 20.5 g

penne with seared tuna & zucchini

This low-fat Mediterranean-style dish with a hint of zesty lemon provides plenty of protein, carbohydrate, niacin, potassium and folate, and some iron and zinc.

400 g (14 oz) penne pasta

oil spray

500 g (1 lb 2 oz) tuna steaks

1 large red onion, cut into thin wedges

2 zucchini (courgettes), sliced into 7 cm (2¾ in) long thin strips

1 clove garlic, chopped

6 small gherkins, rinsed and chopped

1 large handful flat-leaf (Italian) parsley, chopped

zest and juice from 1 large lemon

Prep time: 15 minutes
Cooking time: 20 minutes
Serves 4

Cook the pasta in a large saucepan of boiling salted water for 10 minutes, or until tender. Drain, reserving 250 ml (9 fl oz/1 cup) of the pasta water. Return the pasta to the saucepan.

Meanwhile, pat the fish dry with paper towels. Lightly spray a large, non-stick frying pan with the oil. Heat the oil, add the fish and cook for 2–3 minutes on each side, or until browned on the outside and still pink in the centre. Remove the fish from the pan. Set aside for a few minutes, then cut into 2 cm (¾ in) cubes.

Spray the frying pan with more oil and heat the pan. Add the onion, zucchini and garlic and cook for 2–3 minutes, or until softened. Stir in the gherkins, parsley, lemon zest and juice. Toss into the hot pasta together with the fish and enough of the reserved pasta water to moisten. Serve with a mixed salad.

nutrition per serve Energy 2530 kJ (602 Cal); Fat 9.4 g; Carbohydrate 80.8 g; Protein 44.4 g

spaghettini with ricotta & tuna

The ricotta gives this meal a lovely creamy flavour without the fat. This recipe contains B-group vitamins, antioxidants, potassium, calcium and phosphorus.

375 g (13 oz) spaghettini

4 small ripe tomatoes, peeled and each cut into 8 wedges

3 large handfuls baby rocket (arugula)

2 tsp olive oil

2 cloves garlic, finely chopped

1 long red chilli, seeded and chopped

1 large handful basil

375 g (13 oz/1½ cups) smooth low-fat ricotta

425 g (15 oz) tin tuna in brine or spring water, drained

basil, extra, to serve

grated Parmesan (optional)

Prep time: 15 minutes
Cooking time: 15 minutes
Serves 4

Cook the pasta in a large saucepan of boiling salted water for 10 minutes, or until tender. Drain, reserving 125 ml (4 fl oz/½ cup) of the pasta water. Return the pasta to the saucepan and stir the tomato wedges into the hot pasta.

Set aside about one-quarter of the rocket leaves. Heat the oil in a frying pan, add the garlic and chilli and cook for 1–2 minutes. Add the remaining rocket leaves and cook, stirring, for 1 minute, or until just wilted. Place in a food processor with the basil leaves and ricotta. Process until well combined, adding enough of the reserved pasta water to thin a little.

Toss the ricotta sauce and the reserved rocket leaves through the pasta and tomato wedges. Use a fork to break up the tuna into small chunks and toss through. Garnish with extra basil leaves. Serve with a salad, and grated Parmesan, if you like.

HINT: The easiest way to peel a tomato is to lightly score a cross in the base. Soak the tomato in boiling water for 10–20 seconds, then drain, rinse under cold water and peel the skin away from the cross.

nutrition per serve Energy 2403 kJ (572 Cal); Fat 13.8 g; Carbohydrate 68.4 g; Protein 40.5 g

Rice and noodles are high in carbohydrate and low in fat and can be served with many different types of sauces, as side dishes or main meals. Don't overlook rice just because you think it takes too long to cook. You can use quick-cooking varieties or try a rice cooker to prepare this versatile food ahead of time. Or, why not cook up a large batch and store it in the freezer? It will keep for up to two months.

noodles & rice

noodles with tofu & mushrooms

The marinated tofu blends well with the varied textures of the soba noodles and vegetables. This dish delivers vitamin C, non-haem iron, calcium and phosphorus.

2 tsp sesame oil

3 tbs light soy sauce

2 tbs mirin

2 cloves garlic, finely chopped

2 tsp finely chopped ginger

300 g (10½ oz) packet firm tofu, drained and cut into 3 cm (1¼ in) cubes

280 g (10 oz) packet soba (buckwheat) noodles

115 g (4 oz) fresh baby corn, trimmed

1 tsp canola oil

4 Asian shallots, chopped

150 g (5½ oz) field mushrooms, thickly sliced

300 g (10½ oz/½ bunch) gai larn (Chinese broccoli), trimmed, washed, lightly drained and cut into 5 cm (2 in) pieces

2 tsp sesame seeds, lightly toasted

Prep time: 15 minutes + marinating time

Cooking time: 15 minutes

Serves 4

Combine the sesame oil, soy sauce, mirin, garlic and ginger in a large non-metallic bowl. Add the tofu and gently coat in the marinade. Set aside for at least 15 minutes.

Put the noodles in a large saucepan of cold water and bring to the boil. Add 250 ml (9 fl oz/1 cup) of cold water, bring to the boil again and cook for 5 minutes. Drain. Blanch the corn in a saucepan of boiling water for 2 minutes, refresh and drain.

Heat the canola oil in a large, non-stick wok. Add the Asian shallots and mushrooms and stir-fry for 2–3 minutes. Add the gai larn and corn to the wok with 4 tablespoons water. Stir-fry for a further 2 minutes, or until the gai larn is just wilted. Add the tofu and the marinade; gently stir-fry until combined and heated through. Scatter with sesame seeds and serve on a bed of the noodles.

HINTS: You can use any Asian green vegetable, such as baby bok choy, choy sum or Chinese chard in place of the gai larn.

Mirin is available from supermarkets and Asian stores. Use dry sherry if mirin is not available.

nutrition per serve Energy 1800 kJ (429 Cal); Fat 10.4 g; Carbohydrate 60.9 g; Protein 24.4 g

beef & noodle stir-fry

This nutritious dish is just the thing to give your iron stores and immune system a boost — it provides iron, zinc, vitamin C and other antioxidants.

200 g (7 oz) rice noodles

3 tbs chopped ginger

2 cloves garlic, finely chopped

I tsp sesame oil

2 carrots, cut in half lengthways and thinly sliced

I red capsicum (pepper), quartered, seeded and thinly sliced

100 g (3½ oz/1 cup) snowpeas (mangetout) or sugar snap peas, thinly sliced on an angle

4 spring onions (scallions), sliced

2 tsp canola oil

500 g (1 lb 2 oz) lean beef fillet, cut into strips

I tbs black bean sauce

I tbs oyster or soy sauce

I tbs hoisin sauce or I tsp Chinese five-spice powder

I tbs chilli sauce or ½ large chilli, finely chopped

4 tbs chicken stock or water

4 tbs coarsely chopped coriander (cilantro), stalks included

Prep time: 20 minutes

Cooking time: 10 minutes

Serves 4

Soak the noodles in hot water, immersing them completely. Mix well to break up the noodles and prevent them from sticking together. Leave to soften, then drain just before cooking.

Place the ginger and garlic in a wok. Add the sesame oil on top of the ginger and garlic and turn the heat to high. Cook for about I minute until the wok is hot. Add the vegetables and cook for about 2 minutes, stirring frequently, until tender. Transfer the vegetables to a bowl.

Heat the canola oil in the wok, then add the beef. Cook for I minute, turning the meat over until both sides are just browned. Quickly add the black bean sauce, oyster or soy sauce, hoisin sauce or five-spice powder and chilli sauce or chopped chilli. Mix briefly, then add the meat to the vegetables, leaving behind as much liquid as possible.

Add the drained noodles and the stock or water to the wok, cooking for about I–2 minutes, or until the noodles are soft and tender. Finally, add the beef, vegetables and coriander to the wok, then stir, off the heat, until well mixed. Serve immediately.

nutrition per serve Energy 1702 kJ (405 Cal); Fat 11 g; Carbohydrate 42.2 g; Protein 32 g

spicy chicken stir-fry

Stir-fries are an easy way to include more vegetables in your diet. This pepped-up, tasty dish offers good amounts of antioxidants, B-group vitamins and iron.

4 dried shiitake mushrooms

250 g (9 oz) flat rice stick noodles

oil spray

1 red onion, cut into thin wedges

2 cloves garlic, crushed

2 cm x 2 cm (¾ in x ¾ in) piece fresh ginger, julienned

1 tbs chilli jam

400 g (14 oz) skinless chicken breast fillet, cut into strips

½ red capsicum (pepper), cut into thin strips

800 g (1 lb 12 oz/1 bunch) gai larn (Chinese broccoli), cut into 5 cm (2 in) lengths

115 g (4 oz) fresh or tinned baby corn, halved on the diagonal

150 g (5½ oz/1½ cups) snowpeas (mangetout), halved on the diagonal

4 tbs soy sauce

2 tbs mirin

1 large handful coriander (cilantro) leaves

Prep time: 20 minutes + 15 minutes soaking

Cooking time: 15 minutes

Serves 4

Place the mushrooms in a heatproof bowl and cover with 375 ml (13 fl oz/1½ cups) boiling water and stand for 15 minutes. Drain, reserving the liquid and squeezing out any excess liquid. Remove the stalks and thinly slice the caps. Place the noodles in a heatproof bowl, pour over boiling water to cover and stand for 5 minutes, or until tender. Drain.

Meanwhile, heat a non-stick wok over a high heat and spray with the oil. Add the onion and cook for 2–3 minutes. Add the garlic, ginger and chilli jam and cook for a further 1 minute, adding 1–2 tablespoons of the reserved mushroom liquid to mix in the chilli jam.

Add the chicken and cook for 4–5 minutes, or until almost cooked through. Add the capsicum, gai larn, corn, snowpeas, mushrooms and 3 tablespoons reserved mushroom liquid and stir-fry for 2–3 minutes, or until the vegetables are tender. Add the soy sauce, mirin, coriander and noodles and season with ground white pepper. Toss until well combined and serve immediately.

HINT: Dried shiitake mushrooms, chilli jam and mirin are readily available in supermarkets and Asian food stores.

nutrition per serve Energy 1792 kJ (427 Cal); Fat 7.5 g; Carbohydrate 54 g; Protein 31.5 g

stuffed capsicums

Mediterranean-style flavours enhance the rice, ham and vegetable filling in the baked capsicums. This colourful meal is rich in antioxidants and potassium.

175 g (6 oz) eggplant (aubergine), peeled and diced

1 onion, finely chopped

2 cloves garlic, chopped

400 g (14 oz) tin chopped tomatoes

1 tsp sugar

1 tbs thyme

1 tsp dried oregano

375 g (13 oz/2 cups) cooked brown rice

50 g (1¾ oz) chopped low-fat ham (we used 97% fat-free) (optional)

125 g (4½ oz) tin corn kernels, drained

oil spray

4 red capsicums (peppers), halved and seeded

60 g (2¼ oz/½ cup) grated Cheddar (we used 35% reduced-fat)

Prep time: 25 minutes

Cooking time: 1 hour 5 minutes

Serves 4

Preheat the oven to 180°C (350°F/Gas 4). Place the eggplant, onion, garlic and 125 ml (4 fl oz/½ cup) water in a large, deep, heavy-based frying pan. Bring to the boil, then lower the heat, cover and simmer for 8 minutes, or until softened. Stir once or twice. Remove the lid and simmer until any remaining liquid has evaporated.

Add the tomatoes, sugar and herbs and season well with salt and pepper. Simmer, uncovered, for 8 minutes. Remove from the heat and stir in the rice, ham and corn.

Spray the capsicum shells on the outside with the oil. Fill the capsicum halves with the mixture. Put the capsicums in a large baking dish, pour 250 ml (9 fl oz/1 cup) water into the dish, cover with foil and bake for 45 minutes, or until the capsicums have softened. Remove the foil, sprinkle each capsicum half with grated cheese, bake a further 5 minutes, or until the cheese has melted. Serve with bread to increase your carbohydrate intake and a mixed green salad for extra antioxidants and folate.

HINT: You need 150 g (5½ oz/¾ cup) uncooked brown rice to make 375 g (13 oz/2 cups) cooked brown rice.

nutrition per serve Energy 1242 kJ (296 Cal); Fat 5.4 g; Carbohydrate 44.6 g; Protein 13.6 g

prawn jambalaya

Jambalaya is a versatile Creole dish that combines cooked rice with a variety of vegetables plus any kind of meat, poultry or seafood. This prawn-based version is low in fat and provides good amounts of iodine, selenium and zinc.

1 kg (2 lb 4 oz) large prawns (shrimp), peeled and deveined, heads, shells and tails reserved

2 small onions, chopped

2 sticks celery, chopped

250 ml (9 fl oz/1 cup) dry white wine

1 tbs canola oil

125 g (4½ oz) low-fat bacon, (we used 97% fat-free), thinly sliced

1 red capsicum (pepper), chopped

400 g (14 oz) tin chopped tomatoes

½ tsp cayenne pepper

½ tsp black pepper

¼ tsp dried thyme

¼ tsp dried oregano

400 g (14 oz/2 cups) long-grain rice

Prep time: 25 minutes

Cooking time: 1 hour 10 minutes

Serves 4–6

Put the prawn heads, shells and tails in a saucepan with half the onion, half the celery, the wine and 1 litre (35 fl oz/4 cups) of water. Bring to the boil, then reduce the heat and simmer for 20 minutes. Strain through a fine sieve, reserving the prawn stock.

Heat the oil in a large, heavy-based saucepan and cook the bacon for 3 minutes, or until lightly browned. Remove from the saucepan with a slotted spoon and set aside.

Add the remaining onion, the remaining celery and the capsicum to the saucepan and cook, stirring occasionally, for 5 minutes. Add the tomato, cayenne pepper, black pepper and dried herbs and bring to the boil. Reduce the heat and simmer, covered, for 10 minutes.

Return the bacon to the pan and add the rice and prawn stock. Bring back to the boil, reduce the heat and simmer, covered, for 25 minutes, or until most of the liquid has been absorbed and the rice is tender.

Add the prawns to the saucepan and stir through gently. Cover and cook for another 5 minutes, or until the prawns are pink and cooked through. Serve immediately.

HINT: Prawn heads, shells and tails add extra flavour to stock. If you have to use shelled prawns, enhance the flavour with a good-quality fish stock.

nutrition per serve (6) Energy 1738 kJ (414 Cal); Fat 4.7 g; Carbohydrate 57.8 g; Protein 27.2 g

seafood risotto

If you love seafood, this exceptional dish has it all — well, almost. It also contains carbohydrate, niacin, potassium, phosphorus, iron, zinc and selenium.

12 black mussels

125 ml (4 fl oz/½ cup) white wine

1.5 litres (52 fl oz/6 cups) fish or chicken stock

1 small pinch saffron threads

2 tsp olive oil

8 raw prawns (shrimp), peeled and deveined, tails intact

8 scallops, with coral

3 small squid tubes, cleaned and cut into rings

1 onion, finely chopped

2 cloves garlic, crushed

450 g (1 lb/2 cups) arborio rice

2 tbs chopped flat-leaf (Italian) parsley

Prep time: 25 minutes

Cooking time: 45 minutes

Serves 4

Scrub the mussels with a stiff brush and remove the beards. Discard any broken mussels or any that don't close when tapped. Place the mussels in a heavy-based saucepan with the wine and cook, covered, over a high heat, for 3–4 minutes, or until the mussels have just opened. Remove any that have not opened and discard. Strain and reserve the liquid and set the mussels aside.

Combine the mussel liquid, stock and saffron in a saucepan, cover and keep at a low simmer. Heat 1 teaspoon of the oil in a non-stick pan, over a medium–high heat. Add the prawns and cook until they just turn pink. Remove to a plate, then cook the scallops and squid in batches for 1–2 minutes, or until lightly golden. Remove and set aside with the mussels and prawns.

Heat the remaining teaspoon of oil in a heavy-based saucepan, then add the onion and garlic. Reduce the heat to low and cook for 5–6 minutes, or until soft and translucent. Add the rice and stir until coated. Add 125 ml (4 fl oz/½ cup) of the hot stock, stirring constantly with a wooden spoon until absorbed. Continue adding 125 ml (4 fl oz/½ cup) of liquid at a time, stirring constantly, until all the liquid is absorbed. This should take about 25 minutes. Stir through the seafood and parsley. Season to taste and serve immediately.

nutrition per serve Energy 2641 kJ (629 Cal); Fat 3.6 g; Carbohydrate 93.2 g; Protein 38.3 g

rice & lentil pilaf

This wholesome dish provides fibre, antioxidants, iron and essential amino acids.

200 g (7 oz/1 cup) Puy lentils

2 tsp olive oil

1 small red chilli, seeded and chopped

2 cloves garlic, chopped

2 tsp grated fresh ginger

1 red onion, chopped

1 small red capsicum (pepper), seeded and chopped

1 tsp garam masala

1 tsp ground turmeric

175 g (6 oz/¾ cup) brown rice

1 litre (35 fl oz/4 cups) hot vegetable stock or water

155 g (5½ oz/1 cup) frozen peas, defrosted

Prep time: 10 minutes +
1 hour soaking time
Cooking time: 45 minutes
Serves 4

Put the lentils in a bowl, cover with water and soak for 1 hour. Drain.

Heat the oil in a heavy-based frying pan that is 8 cm (3 in) deep and 24 cm (9½ in) in diameter across the base. Add the chilli, garlic and ginger and cook for 1 minute, then add the onion and capsicum. Cook and stir for 2–3 minutes, or until softened. Add the garam masala and turmeric and cook, stirring, for 1 minute.

Stir in the rice, lentils and hot vegetable stock or water. Continue stirring and bring to the boil. Cover, lower the heat and simmer for 40 minutes, or until the rice and lentils are cooked. Stir in the peas. Serve with a mixed salad.

HINT: Puy lentils are available at most delicatessens. If unavailable, you can use brown lentils.

nutrition per serve Energy 1497 kJ (356 Cal); Fat 5.1 g; Carbohydrate 54.6 g; Protein 18.9 g

fried basmati rice

Low in fat, rich in carbohydrate and big on flavour, this dish is a good meal for topping up your fuel tanks the night before a sporting event.

4 dried shiitake mushrooms

oil spray

2 eggs, lightly beaten

2 tsp canola or olive oil

3 cloves garlic, chopped

1 tbs chopped ginger

1 onion, finely chopped

75 g (2¾ oz) low-fat bacon, (we used 97% fat-free), cut into thin strips

2 tbs Chinese rice wine

1.5 kg (3 lb 4 oz/8 cups) cooked basmati rice

4 French shallots, chopped

155 g (5½ oz/1 cup) frozen peas, defrosted

2 tbs oyster sauce

2 tbs light soy sauce

coriander (cilantro) leaves, to serve

Prep time: 15 minutes + 15 minutes soaking
Cooking time: 10 minutes
Serves 4–6

Cover the mushrooms with boiling water, set aside to soften for 15 minutes. Drain and squeeze dry. Remove the hard stalk, then finely chop. Set aside.

Lightly spray a large wok with the oil spray. Heat the wok and, when hot, add the eggs, swirling around until just set in a thin layer. Use a spatula to roll up the omelette and turn out onto a board. Cut into thin slices and set aside.

Heat the oil in the wok. Add the garlic and ginger and cook for 30 seconds without browning. Add the onion, bacon and mushrooms. Stir-fry for 3 minutes, or until cooked. Stir through the wine.

Add the rice and half of the shallots. Add the peas, oyster sauce, soy sauce and egg slices. Gently stir-fry until heated through. Spoon into 4 serving bowls. Serve with the coriander and remaining shallots.

HINTS: To make about 8 cups of cooked basmati rice you'll need 2 cups uncooked rice.

Chinese rice wine (sometimes labelled Shaoxing) is made from glutinous rice and yeast. It has a rich mellow taste and is used to enhance the flavour in stir-fries and other Chinese dishes. You can use dry sherry in place of the Chinese wine.

nutrition per serve (6) Energy 1725 kJ (411 Cal); Fat 3.6 g; Carbohydrate 78 g; Protein 13 g

chicken & noodles with honey & lime dressing

The secret to this delicious dish is the blending of the Asian flavours in the dressing. It contains folate, potassium, phosphorus, iron and zinc.

DRESSING

3 tbs honey

4 tbs light soy sauce

zest and juice from 2 limes

2 Asian shallots, finely chopped

1 tsp grated fresh ginger

1 small red chilli, seeded and finely chopped

500 g (1 lb 2 oz) Singapore noodles

1 barbecued chicken, skin and fat removed

150 g (5½ oz/1½ cups) snowpeas (mangetout), trimmed and cut in half on the diagonal

180 g (6½ oz/2 cups) bean sprouts

2 sticks celery, cut into thin, 5 cm (2 in) long shreds

2 large handfuls mint

Prep time: 20 minutes

Cooking time: 5 minutes

Serves 4

Combine the dressing ingredients in a small bowl. Place the noodles in a bowl, pour over boiling water and leave for 1 minute to soften. Drain. Refresh under cold water, then cut into short lengths using scissors. Place in a large mixing bowl.

Shred the flesh from the chicken. Blanch the snowpeas in a saucepan of boiling water. Boil for 1 minute, then drain and refresh. Add the snowpeas to the noodles. Add the chicken meat to the noodles.

Add the bean sprouts, celery, mint leaves and dressing and toss well to combine. Serve immediately.

HINTS: You can use any thin noodles. Cook according to the manufacturer's directions.

If you want to reduce the fat in this meal, use freshly cooked chicken meat instead of the barbecued chicken.

nutrition per serve Energy 2120 kJ (505 Cal); Fat 11.5 g; Carbohydrate 53.6 g; Protein 43.5 g

pork & cabbage noodle stir-fry

This is an excellent recipe to add to your weekly menu if you regularly train in the evenings, because it takes so little time to prepare and cook. It is a good source of quality protein, folate, beta-carotene, vitamin C and potassium.

SAUCE

1½ tbs fish sauce

4 tbs light soy sauce

1½ tbs grated palm sugar or soft brown sugar

375 g (13 oz) thin rice stick noodles

2 tsp canola or olive oil

1 onion, finely chopped

2 cloves garlic, finely chopped

1–2 long red chillies, seeded and finely chopped

500 g (1 lb 2 oz) lean minced (ground) pork

1 large carrot, grated

1 zucchini (courgette), grated

225 g (8 oz/3 cups) thinly shredded cabbage

1 large handful coriander (cilantro) leaves

Prep time: 15 minutes
Cooking time: 10 minutes
Serves 4

Combine the sauce ingredients in a small bowl, stirring to dissolve the palm or brown sugar. Place the noodles in a large bowl and cover with boiling water. Set aside for 4 minutes, or until softened. Drain well. Use scissors to cut the noodles into shorter lengths.

Heat the oil in a wok. Add the onion, garlic and chilli and stir-fry for 4 minutes, or until browned and cooked. Break up any lumps as you cook.

Stir in the carrot, zucchini and the cabbage and continue to stir-fry for a further 2–3 minutes, or until the vegetables are just cooked. Stir through the noodles, then the sauce ingredients and coriander leaves.

nutrition per serve Energy 2322 kJ (553 Cal); Fat 12.5 g; Carbohydrate 71.7 g; Protein 34.7 g

pad thai-style rice & prawns

This popular Thai dish has a wonderful aroma and flavour. It provides unsaturated essential fatty acids and minerals such as selenium and iodine.

1 tbs dried shrimp

300 g (10½ oz/1½ cups) jasmine rice

oil spray

2 eggs, lightly beaten

2 tbs light soy sauce

1 tbs fish sauce

1 tbs lime juice

1 tbs grated palm sugar or soft brown sugar

2 tsp canola oil

2 cloves garlic, finely chopped

1 tbs grated fresh ginger

1 long red chilli, seeded and finely chopped

16 cooked prawns (shrimp), peeled and deveined, tails intact

3 spring onions (scallions), chopped

90 g (3¼ oz/1 cup) bean sprouts

1 handful Thai basil, to serve

50 g (1¾ oz/⅓ cup) raw peanuts, lightly roasted and roughly chopped

Prep time: 20 minutes + 15 minutes soaking

Cooking time: 25 minutes

Serves 4

Soak the shrimp in boiling water for 15 minutes. Drain.

Wash the rice in a sieve until the water runs clear. Place in a large saucepan with 750 ml (26 fl oz/3 cups) water. Bring to the boil and boil for 1 minute. Cover tightly, reduce the heat to as low as possible and cook for 10 minutes. Turn off the heat and leave the saucepan covered, for 10 minutes. Fluff the rice with a fork.

Meanwhile, lightly spray a large wok with the oil. Heat the oil and when hot, add the egg, swirling around the wok until just set in a thin layer. Use a spatula to roll up the omelette and turn out onto a board, then cut into thin slices. Set aside.

Combine the soy sauce, fish sauce, lime juice and palm or brown sugar in a bowl and stir to dissolve the sugar.

Heat the oil in the wok. Add the garlic, ginger, chilli and the shrimp and cook for 1 minute, or until aromatic. Stir in the prawns and cook for 1 minute, then add the spring onions, rice and sauce mixture. Stir-fry until well combined and heated through. Stir in the bean sprouts and egg. To serve, scatter with the Thai basil leaves and peanuts.

HINTS: Dried shrimp and palm sugar are available from Asian food stores.

For the best result, cook the rice a day ahead of time or use leftover rice.

nutrition per serve Energy 2029 kJ (483 Cal); Fat 11.7 g; Carbohydrate 67.3 g; Protein 25.3 g

poached salmon kedgeree

A spiced dish combining good-quality protein from eggs and salmon with low-GI carbohydrate from basmati rice. This meal also provides some iron and essential omega-3 fatty acids plus good amounts of niacin and potassium.

2 eggs

750 ml (26 fl oz/3 cups) fish or chicken stock

125 ml (4 fl oz/½ cup) white wine

½ lemon, sliced

2 x 200 g (7 oz) salmon fillets

1 tsp low-fat butter spread

1 large red onion, chopped

2 tbs mild curry powder

2 tsp ground turmeric

325 g (11½ oz/1½ cups) basmati rice

60 g (2¼ oz/½ cup) sultanas

1 large handful flat-leaf (Italian) parsley, finely chopped

1 lemon, cut into 4 wedges, to serve (optional)

ready-made fruit chutney, to serve

Prep time: 20 minutes

Cooking time: 40 minutes

Serves 4

Place the eggs in a saucepan, cover with water and bring to the boil. Boil for 5 minutes, drain and cool quickly in cold water. Peel and chop roughly.

Heat a heavy-based frying pan that is 8 cm (3 in) deep and 24 cm (9½ in) in diameter across the base. Add the stock, wine and lemon slices and heat, then add the fish. Lower the heat and simmer for 8 minutes, or until just cooked through. Place the fish on a plate, remove the skin and roughly flake with a fork. Strain the stock into a jug to measure 750 ml (26 fl oz/3 cups). Set aside. Wipe out the pan.

Heat the butter in the frying pan, add the onion and cook for 2 minutes, or until softened. Add the curry powder, the turmeric and rice. Stir to combine and cook for 1 minute.

Stir in the reserved stock. Bring to the boil, lower the heat, cover and simmer for 20 minutes, or until the rice is cooked and the liquid has been absorbed.

Gently stir the chopped egg, fish, sultanas and half of the parsley through the rice. Top with the remaining parsley and lemon wedges on the side, if using. Serve with the fruit chutney and a salad.

nutrition per serve Energy 2663 kJ (634 Cal); Fat 13.8 g; Carbohydrate 86.1 g; Protein 34.4 g

rice with prawns & vegetables

This delicious and filling paella-style dish is low in fat and rich in low-GI carbohydrate, niacin, folate, beta-carotene, potassium and phosphorus.

2 tsp olive oil

3 cloves garlic, chopped

1 long red chilli, seeded and chopped

2 tsp grated fresh ginger

1 red onion, chopped

1 small red capsicum (pepper), seeded and chopped

400 g (14 oz/2 cups) basmati rice

1 tsp paprika

pinch saffron threads (optional)

125 ml (4 fl oz/½ cup) white wine

1 zucchini (courgette), diced

100 g (3½ oz) button mushrooms, thinly sliced

2 tomatoes, peeled and chopped

1.25 litres (44 fl oz/5 cups) hot vegetable or chicken stock

12 large raw prawns (shrimp), peeled and deveined, tails intact

100 g (3½ oz) low-fat ham (we used 97% fat-free), thickly sliced

130 g (4½ oz/1 cup) frozen peas, defrosted

1 handful flat-leaf (Italian) parsley, chopped, to serve

Prep time: 25 minutes

Cooking time: 40 minutes

Serves 4

Heat the oil in a deep, heavy-based frying pan or paella pan that is 6 cm (2½ in) deep and 30 cm (12 in) in diameter (across the base). Add the garlic, chilli and ginger and cook for 1 minute, or until aromatic. Add the onion and capsicum and cook, stirring, for 2–3 minutes, or until softened.

Stir in the rice, paprika, saffron, if using, and the wine. Cook, stirring until the wine is absorbed. Add the zucchini, mushrooms and tomatoes. Add the hot stock and bring to the boil, stirring continuously. Lower the heat and simmer, uncovered, for 15 minutes. Season to taste.

Arrange the prawns over the rice, pressing a little into the rice. Cover tightly with foil and simmer for 10 minutes, or until the prawns and rice are cooked. Stir in the ham and peas and top with the parsley.

HINT: The easiest way to peel a tomato is to lightly score a cross in the base. Soak the tomato in boiling water for 10–20 seconds, then drain, rinse under cold water and peel the skin away from the cross.

nutrition per serve Energy 2724 kJ (649 Cal); Fat 8.2 g; Carbohydrate 98.2 g; Protein 35.7 g

spring vegetable risotto

This dish needs a lot of stirring to get the lovely creamy texture but it's worth the effort. It contains carbohydrate, niacin, folate, antioxidants and potassium.

250 g (9 oz) cherry tomatoes

3 unpeeled cloves garlic

3 sprigs thyme

oil spray

1.75 litres (61 fl oz/7 cups) chicken or vegetable stock

2 tsp olive oil

1 onion, finely chopped

pinch of salt

450 g (1 lb/2 cups) arborio rice

180 g (6 oz) asparagus, trimmed and cut into 2 cm (½ in) pieces

175 g (6 oz) baby carrots, cut in half on the diagonal

115 g (4 oz/¾ cup) frozen peas, defrosted

2 tbs chopped mint

2 tbs chopped basil

2 tbs chopped flat-leaf (Italian) parsley

30 g (1 oz) Parmesan, grated

Prep time: 20 minutes

Cooking time: 30 minutes

Serves 4

Preheat the oven to 180°C (350°F/Gas 4). Toss the tomatoes in a glass or ceramic ovenproof dish with the unpeeled garlic cloves and thyme. Spray with the oil. Season well, then bake, uncovered, for 30 minutes, or until the tomatoes are soft but still whole.

Meanwhile, pour the stock into a saucepan and bring to the boil. Reduce the heat and keep the stock at a gentle simmer. Heat the oil in a heavy-based saucepan over a medium heat, add the onion and cook, stirring, for 6–7 minutes, or until the onion has softened. Add the rice and stir through for 1 minute, or until well coated.

Add 125 ml (4 fl oz/½ cup) of the hot stock. Cook over a medium heat, stirring constantly, until most of the stock has been absorbed. Continue adding the stock, ½ cup at a time, stirring constantly. After 15 minutes, add the asparagus and carrot, then continue adding the remaining stock until it has all been absorbed and the rice is creamy and tender. Stir through the peas, herbs and Parmesan. Season to taste.

Serve the risotto in individual serving bowls topped with the roasted cherry tomatoes and drizzled with the tomato juice.

nutrition per serve Energy 2791 kJ (664 Cal); Fat 10.7 g; Carbohydrate 112.5 g; Protein 24.8 g

Fish and seafood provide lots of nutrients, such as protein, zinc, iodine and selenium, which the body needs to produce energy and repair any damaged tissues. Seafood and fish are readily available, from fresh and tinned to dried and frozen. If you don't like the taste of fish, try adding tinned tuna or salmon to sandwiches or pasta sauces. Firm fish fillets can be quickly barbecued or stir-fried or made into patties.

fish & seafood

blue-eye cod in chermoula

This low-fat dish is a good choice if you're watching your weight as it contains fish protein, which gives you a feeling of fullness so you don't feel hungry.

CHERMOULA

1½ tbs cumin seeds

2 tsp coriander seeds

1 tbs sweet paprika

pinch cayenne pepper

3 large handfuls coriander (cilantro), chopped

2 large handfuls flat-leaf (Italian) parsley, chopped

4 large cloves garlic, crushed

2 tbs olive oil

4 tbs lemon juice

4 x 150 g (5½ oz) blue-eye cod steaks or other firm white fish steaks

700 g (1 lb 9 oz) small new potatoes

500 g (1 lb 2 oz) zucchini (courgette), thickly sliced

115 g (4 oz) fresh baby corn

Prep time: 20 minutes + 1 hour marinating

Cooking time: 15 minutes

Serves 4

To make the chermoula, place the cumin and coriander seeds, paprika and cayenne pepper in a small, dry frying pan and toast for 1 minute over a medium heat, or until fragrant. Place in a spice grinder, or use a mortar and pestle, and grind to a fine powder. Place in a food processor with the coriander, parsley, garlic, oil and lemon juice. Season well with salt and pepper and process until well combined.

Place the fish in a flat, non-metallic dish and pour over the chermoula. Toss to coat well, cover and marinate in the refrigerator for 1 hour.

Bring a large saucepan of water to the boil and cook the potatoes for 10–12 minutes, or until tender. Steam the zucchini and corn for 3 minutes, or until just cooked.

Meanwhile, remove the fish from the chermoula, reserving the liquid. Heat a chargrill plate or barbecue over a high heat and cook the fish for 2–3 minutes on each side, basting with the remaining chermoula. Serve immediately with the potatoes, zucchini and corn.

HINT: Very active males undertaking regular training and females training at an elite level should increase the amount of potatoes in this recipe or serve the meal with some bread.

nutrition per serve Energy 1635 kJ (389 Cal); Fat 12.1 g; Carbohydrate 32.1 g; Protein 34.6 g

coral trout with garlic tomatoes & gremolata

Strong flavours abound in this tasty, low-fat dish. It is quick to prepare and is a good source of protein, beta-carotene and other antioxidants.

8 vine-ripened tomatoes, halved

12 cloves unpeeled garlic

2 tbs balsamic vinegar

1 tbs soft brown sugar

oil spray

750 g (1 lb 10 oz) new potatoes

300 g (10½ oz) asparagus, trimmed

4 x 200 g (7 oz) coral trout fillets or firm white fish fillets

GREMOLATA

3 handfuls flat-leaf (Italian) parsley, finely chopped

2 tsp lemon zest

2 cloves garlic, finely chopped

Prep time: 20 minutes

Cooking time: 40 minutes

Serves 4

Preheat the oven to 200°C (400°F/Gas 6). Line a large baking tray with baking paper. Place the tomatoes, cut-side-up, on the prepared tray. Scatter around the garlic cloves. Pour over the combined balsamic vinegar and sugar. Spray lightly with the oil. Bake the tomatoes and garlic for 30 minutes, or until softened. Remove the garlic after 15 minutes and baste the tomatoes with the balsamic vinegar and sugar. Squeeze out the soft garlic from the cloves and add to the mushy tomatoes.

Combine the gremolata ingredients in a small bowl.

Bring a large saucepan of water to the boil. Cook the potatoes for 12 minutes, or until cooked when tested with a skewer. Drain. Steam the asparagus for 3–4 minutes, or until just tender.

Pat the fish dry with paper towels. Spray a large, non-stick frying pan with the oil and lightly spray the fish. Cook the fish for 3–4 minutes on each side, or until browned on both sides and just cooked through.

To serve, pile the tomato and garlic onto serving plates. Top with the fish fillets and spoon over some gremolata. Serve with the boiled new potatoes and asparagus to the side.

HINT: Very active people may need to increase the amount of potatoes.

nutrition per serve Energy 1751 kJ (417 Cal); Fat 5 g; Carbohydrate 36.4 g; Protein 48.9

tuna steaks on coriander noodles

This power-packed meal is rich in protein and carbohydrate and it provides healthy monounsaturated fats and essential fatty acids.

3 tbs lime juice

2 tbs fish sauce

2 tbs sweet chilli sauce

2 tsp grated palm sugar or soft brown sugar

1 tsp sesame oil

oil spray

4 x 150 g (5½ oz) tuna steaks, at room temperature

500 g (1 lb 2 oz) dried thin wheat noodles

6 spring onions (scallions), thinly sliced

2 large handfuls coriander (cilantro) leaves, chopped

lime wedges, to serve

Prep time: 15 minutes

Cooking time: 10 minutes

Serves 4

To make the dressing, place the lime juice, fish sauce, chilli sauce, palm or brown sugar and sesame oil in a small bowl and mix together.

Heat a chargrill pan or barbecue and spray with the oil. Add the tuna and cook over a high heat for 2 minutes on each side, or until cooked to your liking. Transfer the steaks to a warm plate, cover and keep warm.

Place the noodles in a large saucepan of lightly salted, rapidly boiling water and return to the boil. Cook for 4 minutes, or until the noodles are tender. Drain well. Add half the dressing and half the spring onions and coriander to the noodles and gently toss together.

Serve the tuna steaks with the noodles. Mix the remaining dressing with the spring onion and coriander and drizzle over the tuna. Serve with the lime wedges.

HINT: You can use salmon steaks instead of the tuna.

nutrition per serve Energy 2963 kJ (706 Cal); Fat 12.6 g; Carbohydrate 90.8 g; Protein 53.2 g

guilt-free fish & chips

This is a healthier, low-fat version of traditional fish and chips. Serve with a fresh mixed salad for extra antioxidants and vitamins.

4 large pontiac potatoes, unpeeled

oil spray

1 tsp sea salt

1 egg white

1 tbs soda water

50 g (1¾ oz/½ cup) dry breadcrumbs

plain (all-purpose) flour, for dusting

4 x 150 g (5½ oz) firm white fish fillets

150 g (5½ oz) baby cos (romaine) lettuce leaves

lemon wedges, to serve

CHEAT'S TARTARE SAUCE

160 g (5¾ oz/⅔ cup) low-fat mayonnaise (we used 97% fat-free)

1 French shallot, finely chopped

1 tbs finely chopped gherkin

1 tbs capers, drained, rinsed and finely chopped

1 tbs finely chopped parsley

2 tsp lemon juice

Prep time: 15 minutes + 30 minutes refrigeration

Cooking time: 45 minutes

Serves 4

Preheat the oven to 200°C (400°F/Gas 6). Cut the potatoes lengthways into wedges. Place the wedges on a non-stick baking tray and spray lightly with the oil. Sprinkle with sea salt and bake for 35–45 minutes, or until evenly golden and crisp, turning halfway through cooking.

Meanwhile, place the egg white and soda water in a shallow dish and whisk until frothy. Put the breadcrumbs in a second shallow dish. Lightly dust the fish fillets with flour. Dip each fillet into the egg white mixture, then coat in the crumbs, shaking off any excess. Place on a plate and refrigerate for 30 minutes while you make the tartare sauce.

To make the tartare sauce, combine all the ingredients in a small, non-metallic serving bowl. Cover and refrigerate until required.

Ten minutes before the wedges are cooked, spray a non-stick frying pan with oil, then heat over a medium–high heat. Cook the fish fillets for 4–5 minutes on each side (depending on their thickness), or until evenly browned and cooked through. Serve the fish and chips with tartare sauce, lettuce leaves and lemon wedges on the side.

HINT: You need firm white fish fillets for this recipe, such as blue-eye cod.

nutrition per serve Energy 1546 kJ (368 Cal); Fat 3.5 g; Carbohydrate 45.7 g; Protein 34.8 g

fish steaks with mushrooms

Tasty and low-fat, this meal is a good source of protein, niacin and potassium. Serve with noodles or rice to add carbohydrate, fibre and B-group vitamins.

2 tbs light soy sauce

I tbs canola oil

2 tbs Chinese rice wine or dry sherry

pinch sugar

zest and juice from I lemon

4 x 200 g (7 oz) snapper steaks

I tsp sesame oil

150 g (5½ oz) fresh shiitake mushrooms, sliced

2 spring onions (scallions), chopped

Prep time: 15 minutes +
4 hours marinating
Cooking time: 35 minutes
Serves 4

Mix the soy sauce, oil, rice wine, sugar, lemon zest and juice together in a jug. Put the fish in a shallow, glass or ceramic ovenproof dish in which they fit snugly in a single layer. Pour the marinade over the fish and turn them once so both sides are coated. Cover and refrigerate for at least 4 hours, or overnight, turning the fish over in the marinade a couple of times.

Remove the fish from the fridge and allow to return to room temperature. Preheat the oven to 180°C (350°F/Gas 4).

Heat the sesame oil in a frying pan over a medium heat and, when hot, add the mushrooms. Cook and stir for 3–4 minutes, or until starting to soften. Add the spring onions, stir and remove from the heat.

Sprinkle the mushroom and onion mixture over the fish and bake, covered with a lid or foil, for 25–30 minutes, or until the fish is opaque and firm to the touch. Serve with egg noodles or rice and green vegetables or salad.

HINTS: You can use swordfish, cod, salmon or halibut steaks in place of the snapper.

Chinese rice wine (sometimes labelled Shaoxing) is available at Asian food stores. If you can't find it, use dry sherry instead.

nutrition per serve Energy 1154 kJ (275 Cal); Fat 8.3 g; Carbohydrate 2.5 g; Protein 44.4 g

marinated & seared tuna with sesame greens

When tuna is marinated and seared as in this dish it retains its moisture and soft texture. It also provides filling lean protein.

4 tbs soy sauce

3 tbs mirin

1 tbs sake

1 tsp caster (superfine) sugar

1 tsp finely grated fresh ginger

2 tsp lemon juice

4 x 175 g (6 oz) tuna steaks

oil spray

350 g (12 oz/1 bunch) choy sum, trimmed and halved

800 g (1 lb 12 oz/1 bunch) gai larn (Chinese broccoli), trimmed and halved

2 tsp sesame seeds, lightly toasted

Prep time: 15 minutes +
30 minutes marinating
Cooking time: 15 minutes
Serves 4

Mix the soy sauce, mirin, sake, sugar, ginger and lemon juice together in a jug. Place the fish in a shallow non-metallic dish and spoon the soy marinade over the top. Turn the fish in the marinade so it is well coated. Cover and leave to marinate for 30 minutes in the fridge.

Preheat a chargrill pan or barbecue until hot and spray with the oil. Lift the fish out of the marinade. Reserve the marinade. Cook the tuna steaks for 1½–2 minutes on each side so that the tuna is cooked on the outside but still pink in the middle.

Pour the marinade into a large frying pan. Bring the liquid to the boil, add the greens and sesame seeds to the simmering sauce, cook and turn until lightly wilted, then place onto serving plates. Top the vegetables with the tuna and the marinade spooned over the top. Serve with rice or noodles.

HINTS: Sake, mirin and sesame oil are available in supermarkets and Asian shops. Use any Chinese-style vegetables such as bok choy, asparagus or broccolini.

You can use salmon in place of the tuna.

nutrition per serve Energy 1418 kJ (338 Cal);
Fat 12.2 g; Carbohydrate 4 g; Protein 48.8 g

chilli squid with asian salad

A quickly prepared meal that provides useful amounts of many vitamins and minerals, including iron, zinc, iodine and selenium.

8 squid

270 g (9¾ oz) packet dried udon noodles

1 small red capsicum (pepper)

3 Asian shallots

200 g (7 oz) baby Asian salad leaves

180 g (6 oz/2 cups) bean sprouts

oil spray

MARINADE

zest and juice from 1 lemon

2 tbs sweet chilli sauce

1 tbs grated palm sugar or soft brown sugar

1 tsp canola oil

LEMON DRESSING

3 tbs lemon juice

3 tbs rice wine vinegar

2 tbs grated palm sugar or brown sugar

1½ tbs fish sauce

1 small red chilli, seeded and chopped

Prep time: 20 minutes + 30 minutes marinating

Cooking time: 15 minutes

Serves 4

To clean the squid, remove the head, insides and the beak. Wash the squid well under cold water and pull away the outer skin. Cut off the tentacles from the heads. Score the skin in a zigzag pattern and cut into 5 cm (2 in) pieces. Combine the marinade in a large, non-metallic bowl, and add the squid pieces and tentacles. Refrigerate for 30 minutes, or longer if possible.

Meanwhile, cook the noodles in a large saucepan of boiling water for 10 minutes, or follow the manufacturer's directions. Drain, then rinse well in cold water and drain again. Cut the noodles into shorter lengths with scissors.

Seed and thinly slice the capsicum. Thinly slice the shallots on the diagonal. Place the salad leaves, capsicum, shallots, bean sprouts and noodles in a serving bowl.

Combine the lemon dressing ingredients in a bowl.

Drain the squid. Heat a barbecue flat plate or frying pan and lightly spray with the oil. Cook and toss the squid over a high heat for 2 minutes, or until cooked.

Add the squid to the salad and toss together with the lemon dressing. Serve immediately.

HINT: To save time, buy squid pieces.

nutrition per serve Energy 1159 kJ (276 Cal); Fat 3.8 g; Carbohydrate 31.6 g; Protein 25.1 g

lemon snapper with potatoes & fennel

The lemon and fennel combo give this dish a delicious aroma. It's also low in fat and is an excellent source of protein, niacin, potassium and phosphorus.

600 g (1 lb 5 oz) potatoes

200 g (7 oz) fennel bulb

3 cloves garlic, crushed

500 ml (17 fl oz/2 cups) chicken stock

1.25 kg (2 lb 12 oz) whole snapper, scaled and cleaned

4 tbs chopped fennel fronds

1 lemon, cut into thin slices

500 g (1 lb 2 oz) broccoli, cut into florets

1 lemon, ½ cut into wedges, ½ juiced

Prep time: 20 minutes

Cooking time: 45 minutes

Serves 4

Preheat the oven to 180°C (350°F/Gas 4). Line a baking tray with baking paper.

Slice the potatoes and fennel as thinly as possible, and layer in a 1.5 litre (52 fl oz/6 cup) glass or ceramic ovenproof dish with the garlic. Bring the chicken stock to the boil, season well and pour over the potato and fennel in the dish. Cook in the oven for 45 minutes, or until the potatoes are soft and the top is golden.

Meanwhile, wash the snapper and pat dry with paper towels. Score the thick part of the flesh in a crisscross pattern. Fill the cavity with the fennel fronds and slices of lemon. Season the skin with sea salt and black pepper. Put the snapper on the prepared tray. Cook in the oven for 25 minutes, or until the flesh has cooked through.

At the same time, steam the broccoli for 3–4 minutes, or until tender.

Remove the fish from the oven, then pour the lemon juice over the fish. Place the fish on a serving platter with the lemon wedges and serve with the broccoli, potato and fennel.

HINTS: You can use any other white-fleshed whole fish.

Very active people should increase the carbohydrates in this meal by serving it with wholegrain bread.

nutrition per serve Energy 1738 kJ (414 Cal); Fat 5.7 g; Carbohydrate 27.3 g; Protein 59.1 g

ginger fish & jasmine rice

This delightfully aromatic meal is low-fat and rich in protein and carbohydrate. Jasmine rice has a high GI; if you want to lower the GI, use basmati.

400 g (14 oz/2 cups) jasmine rice

4 x 300 g (10½ oz) whole snapper or other white-fleshed fish, scaled and cleaned

4 tbs finely chopped ginger

oil spray

1 onion, cut into thin wedges

2 cloves garlic, crushed

1 birdseye chilli, seeded and finely chopped

1 carrot, cut into thick matchsticks

1 small red capsicum (pepper), seeded and julienned

3 tbs chicken stock or water

2 large handfuls snowpea (mangetout) sprouts

1½ tbs soy sauce

½ tsp sesame oil

1 handful coriander (cilantro) sprigs

lime wedges, to serve

Prep time: 20 minutes

Cooking time: 30 minutes

Serves 4

Wash the rice in a sieve until the water runs clear. Place in a large saucepan with 750 ml (26 fl oz/3 cups) water. Bring to the boil and boil for 1 minute. Cover tightly, reduce the heat to as low as possible and cook for 10 minutes. Turn off the heat and leave the saucepan covered for 10 minutes. Fluff the rice with a fork.

Meanwhile, thoroughly wash the fish inside the cavities and out and pat dry with paper towels. Cut 2 diagonal slashes into the thickest part of the fish on both sides. Season the fish with salt and pepper; place ½ tablespoon of the ginger inside the cavities and the rest over the top of the fish.

Line the base of a large bamboo steamer with baking paper or banana leaves. Place the fish in the steamer and place the steamer over a large saucepan or wok of boiling water. Cover and steam for 10–12 minutes, or until the flesh flakes easily when tested with a fork. Remove the fish from the steamer and slide onto the serving plates, pouring any juices over the top of the fish.

Five minutes before the fish is cooked, heat a non-stick wok over a medium–high heat, spray with the oil and add the onion, garlic and chilli. Stir-fry for 2–3 minutes, or until the onion is just beginning to soften, then add the carrot and capsicum. Add the chicken stock and cook, tossing constantly for 2–3 minutes, or until most of the liquid has evaporated. Add the snowpea sprouts, soy sauce and sesame oil and cook for another 1 minute, or until the snowpea sprouts are just beginning to wilt. Top the fish with the vegetables, garnish with the coriander sprigs and serve with the lime wedges and rice.

nutrition per serve Energy 2658 kJ (633 Cal); Fat 5.6 g; Carbohydrate 91.6 g; Protein 51.3 g

salmon with bean purée

This is an excellent recipe for those watching their weight. It contains lean protein, fibre and slowly digested carbohydrate as well as essential fatty acids.

4 x 180 g (6 oz) salmon fillets

2 tsp canola oil

1 clove garlic, crushed

2 tbs white wine vinegar

1 tsp finely grated lime zest

2 tbs chopped fresh dill

600 g (1 lb 5 oz) tin cannellini (white) beans, rinsed and drained

1 bay leaf

250 ml (9 fl oz/1 cup) chicken stock

500 g (1 lb 2 oz/1 bunch) baby English spinach leaves, roughly chopped

Prep time: 15 minutes + 10 minutes marinating

Cooking time: 25 minutes

Serves 4

Place the salmon in a non-metallic dish. Combine the oil, garlic, vinegar, lime zest and dill, pour over the fish, then cover and leave to stand for 10 minutes.

Place the beans, bay leaf and stock in a saucepan, and simmer for 10 minutes. Remove the bay leaf. Place in a food processor and purée. Season well with salt and freshly ground black pepper.

Drain the salmon, reserving the marinade. Cook in a non-stick frying pan over a high heat for 3–5 minutes on each side, or until crisp and golden. Remove, add the marinade to the pan and boil.

Steam the spinach until wilted. Serve the salmon fillets on the purée and spinach and drizzle over the marinade. Serve with chunky slices of brown bread.

nutrition per serve Energy 1770 kJ (421 Cal); Fat 16.6 g; Carbohydrate 16.5 g; Protein 47.6 g

steamed trout with soy, rice wine & ginger

In this delicious dish, the flavours of the trout are enhanced by the soy sauce, ginger and rice wine in which it is gently steamed. It's also low in fat.

2 x 200–225 g (7–8 oz) whole rainbow trout, scaled and cleaned

3 tbs soy sauce

½ tsp sesame oil

I tsp rice or white wine vinegar

2 tsp rice wine or dry sherry

I tbs finely shredded ginger

2 tbs chopped coriander (cilantro)

2 spring onions (scallions), finely chopped

Prep time: 15 minutes

Cooking time: 15 minutes

Serves 2

Rinse the fish and pat dry with paper towels. Score both sides of each fish three times and place the fish in a shallow ovenproof dish.

Mix together the soy sauce, sesame oil, vinegar, rice wine and ginger in a jug. Pour some of the soy sauce mixture inside the fish and then pour the remainder over the fish.

Place the dish in a large bamboo or metal steamer set over a pan of simmering water. Cover and steam for 15 minutes, or until the flesh of the fish is opaque—lift up one side of each fish and look inside to see if the opaqueness has reached the spine. If not, cook until it does.

Take off the lid and scatter the coriander and spring onions over each fish. Serve the fish with rice and steamed Asian greens.

HINT: You can use sea bass or bream in place of the rainbow trout.

nutrition per serve Energy 894 kJ (213 Cal); Fat 7.2 g; Carbohydrate 2.4 g; Protein 32.8 g

fish parcels with vegetables

Here's a great way to have your fish intake all wrapped up in one. This low-fat meal is rich in protein and provides good amounts of most vitamins and minerals.

1.25 kg (2 lb 12 oz) parsnip, peeled and chopped into 5 cm (2 in) chunks

3 tbs skim milk

4 corn cobs, trimmed and each cut into 4 pieces

3 tbs chopped basil

2 cloves garlic, finely chopped

1–2 small red chillies, finely chopped (seeded, optional)

1 tsp grated lemon zest

1 tbs lemon juice

1 tbs olive oil

250 g (9 oz) cherry tomatoes

4 x 200 g (7 oz) skinless firm white fish fillets

1 whole baby fennel bulb, shaved or thinly sliced lengthways

small basil leaves, to serve (optional)

Prep time: 20 minutes

Cooking time: 35 minutes

Serves 4

Preheat the oven to 200°C (400°F/Gas 6). Cook the parsnip in a large saucepan of boiling water for 12 minutes, or until tender. Drain; mash with the milk. Season with sea salt and black pepper. Cook the corn in a saucepan of boiling water for 10 minutes, or until tender. Drain.

Meanwhile, combine the basil, garlic, chilli, zest, lemon juice and olive oil in a small bowl. Season to taste with salt and freshly ground black pepper.

Place the flat blade of a large knife on the cherry tomatoes and gently push until the skins have only just burst.

Place a fish fillet on a sheet of baking or parchment paper big enough to fully enclose it. Smear the fish with 2 teaspoons of the basil mixture. Lay 2–3 slices fennel horizontally on the fillet, then top with a few cherry tomatoes. Bring up two sides of the baking paper, then triple-fold on top to seal. Twist the paper at each end to completely seal. Repeat with remaining fish, marinade, fennel and tomatoes.

Place the fish parcels in a roasting tin and sprinkle with cold water. Roast for 8–12 minutes, or until the fish is cooked through and flakes easily when tested with a fork. Put the fish parcels on serving plates and serve with the parsnip mash, corn and a green salad. The parcels can be opened and garnished with small fresh basil sprigs, if desired.

HINT: You need firm white fish fillets for this recipe, such as blue-eye cod.

nutrition per serve Energy 1745 kJ (415 Cal); Fat 7.5 g; Carbohydrate 40.7 g; Protein 40 g

teriyaki salmon fillets

This dish contains omega-3 fatty acids that can help reduce inflammation. It also provides protein, vitamins and iodine. Serve with rice to add carbohydrate.

4 tbs soy sauce

4 tbs sake

4 tbs mirin

1 tsp sesame oil

2 tbs caster (superfine) sugar

2 tsp finely grated ginger

1 small clove garlic, crushed

4 x 200 g (7 oz) salmon fillets

oil spray

2 spring onions (scallions), chopped

Prep time: 15 minutes + 3 hours marinating

Cooking time: 20 minutes

Serves 4

Mix the soy sauce, sake, mirin, sesame oil, sugar, ginger and garlic together in a jug. Put the fish in a shallow, non-metallic dish and pour the marinade over the top. Turn the fish in the marinade so it is well coated. Cover and leave to marinate in the fridge for at least 3 hours.

Heat a large, heavy-based frying pan and spray with the oil. Lift the fish out of the marinade and drain. Cook the fish for 1–2 minutes, or until browned on each side, then cook at a lower heat for 3 minutes, or until the fish is just cooked through.

Add the marinade and bring to a simmer, then remove the fish and simmer the sauce for 5 minutes, or until thick and sticky. Return the fish to the sauce to coat. Place the fish on a serving plate and pour over the sauce. Garnish with the spring onions and serve with rice.

HINTS: Bottled teriyaki sauces are available from Asian food shops or supermarkets but you will get a much better flavour if you make your own. Use Japanese soy sauce rather than Chinese soy sauce for a full-bodied flavour.

Sake, mirin and sesame oil are available in supermarkets and Asian shops.

nutrition per serve Energy 1598 kJ (381 Cal); Fat 17.7 g; Carbohydrate 10.5 g; Protein 40.4 g

Lean red meat is a good source of iron and zinc, and nutritionists recommend that it is eaten three or four times a week. Meat and poultry can contain significant amounts of fat, but the fat can be minimized by choosing lean cuts and removing the skin from poultry before cooking or serving. Also, try to prepare meat and poultry using low-fat cooking methods, such as dry-baking, stewing and stir-frying.

meat & chicken

herb-crusted lamb roast with vegetables

A more flavoursome version of the traditional lamb roast with vegetables, this dish is loaded with iron, zinc, beta-carotene, folate and B-group vitamins.

6 large carrots, cut into 2 cm (¾ in) pieces on the diagonal

oil spray

2 tbs Dijon mustard

2 tbs finely chopped flat-leaf (Italian) parsley

1 tsp finely chopped thyme

1 tsp finely chopped sage

3 cloves garlic, crushed

2 x 300 g (10½ oz) pieces lamb rump or mini lamb roasts, trimmed

750 g (1 lb 10 oz) small new potatoes

250 ml (9 fl oz/1 cup) vegetable stock

620 g (1 lb 6 oz/4 cups) frozen peas

2 tbs mint

Prep time: 20 minutes

Cooking time: 1 hour

Serves 4

Preheat the oven to 200°C (400°F/Gas 6). Spray the carrots with the oil, season well and place into a large roasting tin (you will be adding the lamb pieces halfway through cooking). Cook in the oven for 1 hour, or until golden and soft.

Place the mustard, parsley, thyme and 2 of the crushed garlic cloves in a bowl. Mix well to combine and add the lamb pieces. Thoroughly coat with the mixture and add to the carrots in the roasting tin 30 minutes before it is due to be ready.

Meanwhile, cook the potatoes in a large saucepan of boiling water for 12 minutes, or until tender. Drain.

In a small saucepan over high heat, bring the vegetable stock to the boil, with the remaining crushed garlic clove. Add the peas and cook for 3 minutes. Remove from the heat and strain, reserving the stock. Put the peas, mint and reserved stock in a food processor. Blend until smooth, and season well to taste.

Remove the lamb from the oven and allow to rest, covered, on a board for 5 minutes, before slicing across the grain. Serve with the potatoes, pea and mint pureé and the roasted carrots.

nutrition per serve Energy 2089 kJ (497 Cal); Fat 11.2 g; Carbohydrate 43.5 g; Protein 48.6 g

steak sandwich with onion relish

This is one hearty (and tasty) sandwich that's packed with lots of nutrients, such as protein, niacin, phosphorus and easily absorbed zinc and iron.

RED ONION RELISH
1 tsp olive oil
2 red onions, thinly sliced
2 tbs soft brown sugar
2 tbs balsamic vinegar
1 tbs thyme

250 g (9 oz) mixed mushrooms (flat, button, shiitake), sliced
oil spray
4 lean minute beef steaks, trimmed
3 large handfuls baby English spinach leaves
ciabatta or sourdough bread

Prep time: 20 minutes
Cooking time: 25 minutes
Serves 4

To make the red onion relish, heat the oil in a saucepan. Add the onion and cook over a low heat for 10 minutes, or until softened, taking care not to burn. Add the sugar and balsamic vinegar. Cook and stir often over a low heat for 10–12 minutes, or until softened and slightly syrupy. Stir in the thyme.

Meanwhile, place the mushrooms and 125 ml (4 fl oz/½ cup) water in a heavy-based frying pan. Bring to the boil, stirring to coat the mushrooms in the water. Simmer, covered, for 5 minutes, or until softened, making sure the mushrooms don't dry out. Stir once or twice. Remove the lid and increase the heat to allow the juice to evaporate. Season well with salt and freshly ground black pepper.

Lightly spray a chargrill pan or frying pan with the oil. Add the meat and cook for 1 minute on each side, or until cooked to your liking.

Very briefly microwave or steam the spinach until just wilted. Drain away any juices.

Slice the bread on the diagonal into 8 thick slices and toast. To serve, arrange 2 slices of bread on each plate. Top with the spinach, then the steak and mushrooms and finish with a dollop of the relish. Serve with a mixed salad to boost your intake of antioxidants.

HINT: For full flavour, use at least two varieties of mushrooms.

nutrition per serve Energy 1748 kJ (416 Cal); Fat 10.2 g; Carbohydrate 41.8 g; Protein 36.1 g

chicken pot pies with wedges

This reduced-fat version of chicken pie and chips contains lots of carbohydrate and many vitamins and minerals. Use ready-made puff pastry if you're rushed.

oil spray

2 leeks, thinly sliced

3 large cloves garlic, crushed

400 g (14 oz) chicken breast fillet, trimmed and cut into 1.5 cm (¾ in) pieces

300 g (10½ oz) button mushrooms, quartered

3 tbs plain (all-purpose) flour

500 ml (17 fl oz/2 cups) chicken stock

2 x 125 g (4½ oz) tins corn kernels, drained

2 potatoes, cut into 1 cm (½ in) cubes

2 tsp finely chopped oregano

1 kg (2 lb 4 oz) desiree potatoes, cut into small wedges

PASTRY

185 g (6¼ oz/1½ cups) self-raising flour

20 g (¾ oz) butter

100 ml (3½ fl oz) low-fat milk

Prep time: 30 minutes

Cooking time: 1 hour 5 minutes

Serves 4

Preheat the oven to 200°C (400°F/Gas 6). Spray a non-stick frying pan with the oil and heat over a medium heat.

Add the leeks and cook for 2–3 minutes, or until softened. Add the garlic and cook for 30 seconds. Set aside. Increase the heat to high and cook the chicken for 4–5 minutes, or until cooked. Return the leek mixture to the pan, add the mushrooms and cook for 2 minutes, or until softened. Stir in the flour and cook for 1 minute, then gradually add the stock, stirring continuously. Add the corn and potatoes and cook for 10 minutes, or until thickened. Stir through the oregano and season. Spoon into four 375 ml (13 fl oz/1½ cup) ovenproof dishes.

Place the potato wedges in a non-stick baking tray and spray with oil. Sprinkle with sea salt and bake for 40 minutes, turning halfway through, or until golden and cooked through.

To make the pastry, sift the flour into a bowl, rub in the butter with your fingertips, then make a well in the centre. Combine 4 tablespoons of the milk with 4 tablespoons water and add enough to the dry ingredients to make a soft dough. Turn out onto a floured surface and bring together to form a smooth dough. Cut into 4 portions and roll out each one so it is 1 cm (½ in) larger than the top of the dish. Brush the edge of the dough with the remaining milk and place over each dish, pressing the edges to seal. Brush the tops with milk and make a small slit in the top of each pie.

Bake for 20–25 minutes, or until the pastry is golden and puffed. Serve with the potato wedges.

nutrition per serve Energy 2826 kJ (673 Cal); Fat 12.8 g; Carbohydrate 89.2 g; Protein 42.4 g

cajun chicken with salsa

Savour the flavours of this exotic dish and also know that you're getting a good serve of antioxidants and protein as well as B-group vitamins.

4 sweet potatoes, peeled and cut into 3 cm (1¼ in) chunks

oil spray

4 skinless chicken thighs on the bone

4 skinless chicken drumsticks

3 tbs Cajun seasoning

lime wedges, to serve

SALSA

3 cobs sweet corn

1 Lebanese (short) cucumber, cut into 5 mm (¼ in) dice

2 vine-ripened tomatoes, cut into 5 mm (¼ in) dice

1 small handful coriander (cilantro) leaves, roughly chopped

2 tbs lime juice

1 tsp fish sauce

Prep time: 25 minutes

Cooking time: 50 minutes

Serves 4

Preheat the oven to 180°C (350°F/Gas 4). Spray the sweet potatoes with the oil and season. Place in a roasting tin and roast in the oven for 40–45 minutes, or until golden and cooked through.

Put the chicken in a large bowl, add the Cajun seasoning mix and toss together well until the pieces are evenly coated. Place into a roasting tin and roast in the oven for 45 minutes, or until cooked through.

To make the salsa, cook the corn in a saucepan of boiling water for 8 minutes. Drain and refresh under cold water. Remove the kernels, using a sharp knife, and place in a bowl with the cucumber, tomato, coriander, lime juice and fish sauce. Mix together and season to taste.

Serve the chicken pieces with the roasted sweet potato, the salsa and lime wedges.

nutrition per serve Energy 1693 kJ (403 Cal); Fat 9 g; Carbohydrate 41.7 g; Protein 33.6 g

shepherd's pie

A reduced-fat version of an old favourite, this pie is both hearty and nutritious. It provides iron and zinc, B-group vitamins, potassium and beta-carotene.

1 kg (2 lb 4 oz) potatoes
6 large cloves garlic, peeled
4 tbs skim milk
oil spray
1 large onion, finely chopped
3 large cloves garlic, crushed
2 sticks celery, finely chopped
2 carrots, diced
750 g (1 lb 10 oz) lean minced (ground) lamb
1½ tbs plain (all-purpose) flour
2 tbs tomato paste (purée)
2 tsp chopped thyme
2 tsp chopped rosemary
2 bay leaves
315 ml (10¾ fl oz/1¼ cups) beef stock
1 tbs Worcestershire sauce
pinch ground nutmeg

Prep time: 20 minutes
Cooking time: 45 minutes
Serves 6

Preheat the oven to 180°C (350°F/Gas 4). Cut the potatoes into chunks and cook in a large saucepan of boiling water with the whole garlic cloves for 10–15 minutes, or until tender. Drain well and return to the saucepan. Mash the potato and garlic with a potato masher until smooth. Stir through the milk and season with salt and freshly ground black pepper.

Meanwhile, lightly spray a large, non-stick frying pan with the oil and heat over a medium heat. Add the onion, crushed garlic, celery and carrot and cook for 5 minutes, or until the vegetables begin to soften (add water if needed). Remove from the pan.

Add the lamb and cook over a high heat until well browned, breaking up any lumps with the back of a spoon. Add the flour and cook for 1–2 minutes. Return the vegetables to the pan with the tomato paste, herbs, bay leaf, stock, sauce and nutmeg and bring to the boil. Reduce the heat and simmer for 5 minutes, or until thickened.

Pour the lamb mixture into a 2 litre (70 fl oz/4 cup) ovenproof dish. Spoon the potato over the top, smoothing the surface, then fluff with a fork. Bake for 25–30 minutes, or until lightly golden and crusty. Serve with salad and bread.

HINT: The potato will not turn as brown as a regular shepherd's pie, because there is less fat in this recipe.

nutrition per serve Energy 1445 kJ (344 Cal); Fat 9.7 g; Carbohydrate 29.3 g; Protein 32 g

thai chicken burgers

These Eastern-style burgers are deliciously different from the commercial versions. They also have less fat and more nutrients, such as antioxidants.

400 g (14 oz) lean minced (ground) chicken

80 g (2¾ oz/1 cup) fresh breadcrumbs

1 clove garlic, crushed

1 large handful coriander (cilantro) leaves, chopped, plus 1 tbs, extra

3 tbs sweet chilli sauce

1 tsp ground coriander

3 spring onions (scallions), finely chopped

60 g (2¼ oz/¼ cup) sugar

2 tbs white vinegar

2 tbs finely chopped raw or dry-roasted peanuts

1 large carrot

1 large Lebanese (short) cucumber

oil spray

4 hamburger or wholegrain buns

2 handfuls mixed lettuce leaves

1 vine-ripened tomato, sliced

Prep time: 25 minutes + 30 minutes refrigeration
Cooking time: 15 minutes
Serves 4

Put the chicken, breadcrumbs, garlic, fresh coriander, chilli sauce, ground coriander and spring onion in a large bowl, and mix together with your hands. Shape into 4 patties. Refrigerate, covered, for 30 minutes.

To make the dressing, put the sugar, vinegar and 3 tablespoons water in a small saucepan, and stir over low heat until the sugar dissolves. Simmer for 5 minutes, or until slightly thickened. Cool and stir in the peanuts and extra coriander.

Peel strips of carrot and cucumber to make 'ribbons'.

Heat a chargrill plate or barbecue, spray with the oil and cook the burgers for 4 minutes on each side, or until tender. Serve on hamburger buns, with the dressing, lettuce, tomato, carrot and cucumber.

HINT: To save time in the evening, make a batch of the chicken patties on the weekend and freeze them individually. Pull them out when you are ready to eat them. They will freeze for 1 month.

nutrition per serve Energy 2100 kJ (500 Cal); Fat 14.2 g; Carbohydrate 60.3 g; Protein 29.7 g

moroccan chicken on couscous

Aromatic and tasty, this meal contains vitamins, protein, fibre, iron and zinc.

1 tsp dried cumin seeds
1 tsp dried coriander seeds
1 tsp ground ginger
1 tsp ground turmeric
1 tsp ground cinnamon
½ tsp chilli flakes
8 skinless chicken pieces
3 tsp olive oil
1 onion, finely chopped
3 cloves garlic, crushed
1 tsp finely grated ginger
400 g (14 oz) tin chopped tomatoes
250 ml (9 fl oz/1 cup) chicken stock

COUSCOUS

375 ml (13 fl oz/1½ cups) chicken stock
1 clove garlic, crushed
3 spring onions (scallions)
280 g (10 oz) couscous
400 g (14 oz) tin chickpeas
2 tbs finely chopped coriander (cilantro)

Prep time: 20 minutes + 15 minutes standing
Cooking time: 1 hour
Serves 4

In a small, heavy-based frying pan, place the cumin and coriander seeds, ginger, turmeric, cinnamon and chilli flakes. Cook, stirring, over a medium heat for 1 minute, or until fragrant. Grind, using a mortar and pestle or spice grinder to make a powder.

Sprinkle the chicken pieces with the spice mix, rubbing in well. In a large, deep, heavy-based frying pan, heat 2 teaspoons of the oil. Add the chicken pieces and cook for 8 minutes, turning so the pieces brown evenly. Remove from the pan and set aside.

In the same pan, add the remaining oil and, over a medium heat, cook the onion, garlic and ginger for 3 minutes, or until softened. Add the chopped tomatoes, stock and return the chicken to the pan. Bring to the boil, reduce the heat to low, cover and simmer for 45 minutes, or until the chicken is tender and the sauce reduced. Season to taste.

Meanwhile, to make the couscous, in a small saucepan bring the chicken stock and the garlic to the boil. Put the couscous in a non-metallic bowl and pour over the hot stock. Cover with plastic wrap and sit for 15 minutes. Finely chop the spring onions on the diagonal. Stir the couscous with a fork, then add the rinsed and drained chickpeas, coriander and spring onions. Season well. Serve on a platter topped with the Moroccan chicken, sprinkled with chopped coriander.

HINT: We used skinless chicken thighs with the bone, plus drumsticks. To reduce the amount of fat in the meal, use 8 chicken drumsticks—they have less fat than chicken thighs.

nutrition per serve Energy 3000 kJ (714 Cal); Fat 25.4 g; Carbohydrate 72.4 g; Protein 55.5 g

green chicken curry

All the flavour of a rich curry minus the high fat content. This nutritious meal also provides good amounts of protein, B-group vitamins and minerals.

250 g (9 oz/1¼ cups) jasmine rice

oil spray

1 onion, cut into thin wedges

2 cloves garlic, crushed

2 tbs finely chopped coriander (cilantro) roots and stems

1 tbs green curry paste

2 skinless chicken breast fillets, cut into thin strips

375 ml (13 fl oz/1½ cups) evaporated reduced-fat milk

170 ml (5½ fl oz/⅔ cup) light coconut milk

6 kaffir lime leaves

125 g (4½ oz) snake beans, cut into 3 cm (1¼ in) lengths

300 g (10½ oz) broccoli, cut into small florets

1 tbs shaved palm sugar or soft brown sugar

2–3 tbs fish sauce

1 large handful coriander (cilantro) leaves

Prep time: 20 minutes + 10 minutes standing
Cooking time: 20 minutes
Serves 4

Rinse the rice and place in a saucepan. Add 425 ml (15 fl oz/1¾ cups) water and bring to the boil. Cover, reduce the heat to very low and cook for 10 minutes. Remove from the heat and leave to stand, covered, for 10 minutes.

Meanwhile, spray a non-stick wok with the oil, heat over a high heat and cook the onion for 2–3 minutes, or until softened. Add the garlic, coriander roots and stems and curry paste and cook for 1 minute. Add the chicken and stir-fry for 3–4 minutes, or until almost cooked through.

Stir through the evaporated milk, coconut milk, lime leaves, beans and broccoli and cook for 4–5 minutes, or until the chicken and vegetables are cooked. Stir in the palm sugar, fish sauce and coriander. Season to taste with salt and freshly ground black pepper. Serve with the steamed rice.

HINT: Jasmine rice has a high GI value. If you want to lower the GI value, you can use basmati rice.

nutrition per serve Energy 2493 kJ (593 Cal); Fat 16.8 g; Carbohydrate 67.2 g; Protein 40.3 g

red curry pork & bean stir-fry

This quick and easy meal provides good amounts of protein, B-group vitamins, antioxidants and a range of minerals, including easily absorbed iron and zinc.

400 g (14 oz/2 cups) jasmine rice, washed and drained

125 g (4½ oz) green beans, trimmed and cut into 4 cm (1½ in) lengths

100 g (3½ oz) sugar snap peas

1 tsp canola oil

4 Asian shallots, thinly sliced

2 cloves garlic, crushed

1–1½ tbs red curry paste

400 g (14 oz) lean pork fillet, thinly sliced

1½ tbs fish sauce

1 tbs palm sugar or soft brown sugar

3 kaffir lime leaves (optional)

Prep time: 20 minutes
Cooking time: 25 minutes
Serves 4

Bring a large saucepan of water to the boil and stir in the rice. Boil rapidly for 15 minutes, occasionally stirring with a fork. Drain, rinse with hot water and drain again.

Meanwhile, place the beans and peas in a saucepan of boiling water. Blanch for 2 minutes, then rinse under cold water and drain. Set aside.

Heat the oil in a large wok. Add the shallots and garlic and cook, stirring, for 1 minute. Stir in the curry paste, to taste, and cook for a further 1 minute.

Increase the heat to high and add the pork all at once. Stir-fry for 2–3 minutes, or until the pork has just changed colour. Lower the heat and add the fish sauce, palm sugar or brown sugar, 4 tablespoons water, the beans, peas and kaffir lime leaves, if using. Stir to heat through, then serve with the rice.

HINT: Jasmine rice has a high GI value. If you're watching your weight or your blood sugar level, use basmati rice instead of jasmine.

nutrition per serve Energy 2180 kJ (519 Cal); Fat 5 g; Carbohydrate 85.6 g; Protein 30.9 g

tandoori chicken skewers & rice

This delightfully spicy dish is big on flavour and blends well with the rice. It's also rich in carbohydrate and protein and has many vitamins and minerals.

1½ tbs tandoori spice powder

125 g (4½ oz/½ cup) low-fat plain yoghurt

1 tbs lemon juice

4 x 200 g (7 oz) skinless chicken fillets, cut into 2 cm (¾ in) strips

300 g (10½ oz/1½ cups) basmati rice

2 tsp oil

1 small onion, finely diced

2 cloves garlic, crushed

1 tsp ginger, finely grated

½ tsp ground turmeric

1 tsp cumin seeds

4 bruised cardamom pods

1 stick cinnamon

500 ml (17 fl oz/2 cups) chicken stock

2 tbs currants

oil spray

mango chutney, lemon wedges and coriander (cilantro), to serve

Prep time: 20 minutes + 2 hours marinating

Cooking time: 15 minutes

Serves 4

Soak 8 bamboo skewers in cold water for 30 minutes. Place the spice powder, yoghurt, lemon juice and chicken in a non-metallic bowl. Mix well to combine, then cover and refrigerate for 2 hours.

For the pilaf, rinse the rice under cold water until it runs clear. Heat the oil over a medium heat in a saucepan, add the onion, garlic, ginger, turmeric and cumin seeds. Cook for 5 minutes, or until softened, and then add the rice, cardamom, cinnamon and chicken stock.

Bring to the boil, reduce the heat to low, cover and cook for 12 minutes. Remove from the heat, add the currants and stir through. Season well with salt and freshly ground pepper and set aside, covered, for 10 minutes before serving.

Meanwhile, weave the chicken pieces onto the skewers so they are evenly distributed, but not too close together. Heat a chargrill pan or frying pan over a medium heat and spray with the oil. Add the skewers, and cook for 12–15 minutes, turning, so that they cook evenly. Serve the skewers on the rice pilaf with mango chutney, lemon wedges and coriander leaves.

HINT: If you train in the evenings, save time by marinating the chicken in the morning and leaving it in the fridge all day.

nutrition per serve Energy 2778 kJ (661 Cal); Fat 15.9 g; Carbohydrate 73.2 g; Protein 53.8 g

coq au vin with potato & greens

This low-fat version of the classic dish contains many vitamins and minerals.

2 tsp oil

3 cloves garlic, chopped

125 g (4½ oz) lean bacon, thickly sliced

8 skinless chicken drumsticks

12 baby onions, peeled

2 tbs plain (all-purpose) flour

500 ml (17 fl oz/2 cups) red wine

2 tbs brandy

310 ml (11 fl oz/1¼ cups) chicken stock

2 bay leaves

3 sprigs thyme

200 g (7 oz) button mushrooms, halved

1 kg (2 lb 4 oz) desiree potatoes, cut into 4 cm (1½ in) pieces

4 tbs skim milk

1 handful flat-leaf (Italian) parsley, chopped

160 g (5¾ oz/1 cup) peas

100 g (3½ oz/1 cup) snowpea (mangetout) sprouts, trimmed

100 g (3½ oz/1 cup) sugar snap peas, trimmed

Prep time: 25 minutes

Cooking time: 2 hours 20 minutes

Serves 4

Preheat the oven to moderate 180°C (350°F/Gas 4). Heat the oil in a flameproof casserole dish over a high heat. Add the garlic and bacon and cook for 2–3 minutes, or until lightly golden. Remove from the dish. Add the chicken and cook for 4–5 minutes, or until browned. Remove the chicken. Add the onions and cook, turning, for 2–3 minutes, or until golden. Remove from the heat.

Stir the flour into the dish and slowly pour in the wine and brandy, stirring constantly to prevent lumps from forming. Return to the heat and cook over a high heat for 2–3 minutes. Add the stock, bay leaves and thyme and bring to the boil over a high heat.

Return the garlic, bacon, chicken and onion to the casserole. Cover and cook in the oven for 1 hour 20 minutes. Add the mushrooms to the casserole and cook, covered, in the oven for a further 30 minutes.

Meanwhile, bring a large saucepan of water to the boil and cook the potatoes for 15 minutes, or until tender. Drain and mash with a potato masher, until smooth. Stir through the milk until smooth and fluffy, add the parsley and season with salt and ground black pepper.

Put the peas into a saucepan of boiling water. Cook for 3 minutes, add the snowpea sprouts and sugar snap peas and cook for a further 1 minute. Drain. Season with salt and freshly ground black pepper and serve with the mashed potato and greens.

HINTS: We used 97% fat-free bacon.

This is a great dish to make on the weekend and reheat during the week.

nutrition per serve Energy 2857 kJ (680 Cal); Fat 15.5 g; Carbohydrate 52 g; Protein 52.4 g

beef skewers with salad & rice

This carb-rich dish is loaded with folate, potassium, antioxidants and more!

600 g (1 lb 5 oz), lean beef sirloin steaks

1 large red capsicum (pepper)

400 g (14 oz/2 cups) basmati rice, washed and drained

6 x 4 cm (1¾ in) flat or button mushrooms

oil spray

1 tbs sesame seeds, toasted

MARINADE

3 tbs teriyaki sauce

2 tbs honey

1 tsp olive oil

2 cloves garlic, crushed

TOMATO MINT SALAD

4 vine-ripened tomatoes, seeded and chopped

3 spring onions (scallions), chopped

1 Lebanese (short) cucumber, seeded and chopped

2 handfuls mint, chopped

2 tbs fat-free dressing

Prep time: 25 minutes + soaking and marinating time

Cooking time: 25 minutes

Serves 4

Soak 8 long wooden skewers in water for 15 minutes. Cut the meat into bite-sized cubes. Seed the capsicum, then cut into 24 x 3 cm (1¼ in) cubes. Thread the meat onto the skewers, alternating with the mushrooms and capsicum.

Combine the marinade ingredients in a non-metallic flat dish. Lay the skewers in the marinade and coat well. Refrigerate for at least 20 minutes, turning in the marinade occasionally.

Combine the tomato mint salad ingredients in a bowl.

Bring a large saucepan of salted water to the boil and stir in the rice. Boil, uncovered, for 15 minutes, or until tender. Drain, rinse under hot water, then drain again.

Meanwhile, preheat a grill (broiler) or barbecue, cook and turn the skewers, spraying lightly with the oil, for 8 minutes, or until just cooked. Brush 2 or 3 times with the remaining marinade. Take care not to overcook or they will dry out.

Scatter over the sesame seeds. Serve the skewers on a bed of rice with the tomato mint salad to the side.

HINT: You can also use Swiss brown or shiitake mushrooms in this recipe.

nutrition per serve Energy 2941 kJ (700 Cal); Fat 13.4 g; Carbohydrate 99.4 g; Protein 42.3 g

beef rolls in tomato sauce

This hearty and filling dish contains iron, zinc, phosphorus, vitamins and protein. The sweet potato has a lower GI than mashed potato.

TOMATO SAUCE

oil spray

1 onion, finely chopped

1 stick celery, finely chopped

125 ml (4 fl oz/½ cup) red wine

2 x 400 g (14 oz) tins chopped tomatoes

2 tbs tomato paste (pureé)

2 tsp sugar

2 sprigs thyme

PARSLEY STUFFING

1 large handful flat-leaf (Italian) parsley, chopped

45 g (1½ oz/½ cup) grated Parmesan

3 cloves garlic, finely chopped

zest of 2 large lemons

8 x 85 g (3 oz) minute steaks

850 g (1 lb 14 oz) purple sweet potato, peeled and cut into 5 cm (2 in) pieces

3 tbs skim milk

shredded herbs, to serve

Prep time: 30 minutes

Cooking time: 1¼ hours

Serves 4

Heat a heavy-based frying pan that is 8 cm (3 in) deep and 24 cm (9½ in) in diameter (across the base) and spray with the oil. Cook the onion and celery for 2–3 minutes, or until softened. Add the wine and cook until the wine is reduced by two-thirds. Add the tomatoes, tomato paste, sugar and thyme sprigs. Add 500 ml (17 fl oz/2 cups) water, stir and simmer, uncovered, stirring occasionally, for 30 minutes, or until thickened and reduced. Remove the thyme sprigs.

Meanwhile, combine the parsley, cheese, garlic and lemon zest in a bowl. Flatten the steaks with a meat mallet to an even 5 mm (¼ in) thick. Pat dry with paper towels. Divide the parsley stuffing evenly over the steaks. Roll up firmly and secure each with a toothpick.

Spray a large, non-stick frying pan with oil. Brown the beef rolls all over, then transfer to the tomato sauce. Arrange in a single layer. Bring to the boil, then lower the heat, cover and simmer for 45 minutes, or until tender. Turn once or twice during cooking.

Meanwhile, place the sweet potato in a saucepan of boiling water. Cook for 15 minutes, or until tender, then drain. Add the milk and use a flat-sided dinner knife to roughly chop.

Serve two beef rolls per person and spoon over the sauce. Top with the shredded herbs. Serve with the sweet potato mash and a mixed salad on the side.

nutrition per serve Energy 2146 kJ (511 Cal); Fat 12.5 g; Carbohydrate 42.5 g; Protein 47.6 g

moussaka with chickpea salad

This low-fat version of a Greek favourite makes a nourishing, low-GI meal.

1 kg (2 lb 4 oz) eggplant (aubergine)

oil spray

2 onions, finely chopped

3 large cloves garlic, crushed

½ tsp ground allspice

1 tsp ground cinnamon

500 g (1 lb 2 oz) lean minced (ground) lamb

2 tbs tomato paste (purée)

125 ml (4 fl oz/½ cup) red wine

2 x 400 g (14 oz) tins tomatoes

3 tbs chopped parsley

90 g (3¼ oz) low-fat Cheddar

20 g (¾ oz) butter

40 g (1½ oz/⅓ cup) flour

375 ml (13 fl oz/1½ cups) skim milk

150 g (5½ oz/⅔ cup) low-fat ricotta

pinch ground nutmeg

425 g (15 oz) tin chickpeas

½ red onion

3 handfuls rocket (arugula)

2 tbs ready-made fat-free dressing

Prep time: 30 minutes

Cooking time: 1½ hours

Serves 6

Preheat the oven to 180°C (350°F/Gas 4). Cut the eggplant into 5 mm (¼ in) thick slices. Spray the eggplant with the oil and grill (broil) under a preheated grill (broiler) for 4 minutes on each side, or until golden.

Heat a large, non-stick saucepan and lightly spray with oil. Cook the onions for 3–4 minutes, or until softened. Add the garlic, allspice and cinnamon and cook for 1 minute.

Add the lamb and cook for 3–4 minutes, or until cooked. Add the tomato paste, wine and tomatoes. Bring to the boil, then reduce the heat and simmer for 30–35 minutes, stirring occasionally, or until most of the liquid has evaporated. Stir in the parsley and season to taste.

To make the white sauce, grate the cheese. Melt the butter in a saucepan over a medium heat. Stir in the flour and cook for 1 minute. Remove from the heat and gradually stir in the milk. Return to the heat and stir constantly until the sauce boils and thickens. Reduce the heat and simmer for 2 minutes. Stir through the ricotta and nutmeg until smooth and season to taste.

Spoon half the meat sauce over the base of a 3 litre (105 fl oz/12 cup) 25 x 30 cm (10 x 12 in) ovenproof dish. Cover with half of the eggplant. Spoon over the remaining meat sauce and cover with the remaining eggplant. Spread over the sauce and sprinkle with the cheese. Bake for 30 minutes, or until golden. Stand for 5 minutes before serving.

To make the salad, rinse and drain the chickpeas. Cut the onion into thin wedges. Put the rocket, onion and chickpeas in a bowl. Add the dressing, season with salt and pepper and toss until well combined.

nutrition per serve Energy 1748 kJ (416 Cal); Fat 15.7 g; Carbohydrate 26.9 g; Protein 34.5 g

pork & bean chilli with rice

This nutritious meal is delicious served freshly cooked or reheated the following day when the flavours have had time to enrich the chilli.

PORK AND BEAN CHILLI

oil spray

600 g (1 lb 5 oz) lean pork fillet

1 small red onion, finely chopped

3 cloves garlic, finely chopped

1½ tsp ground cumin

1 tsp ground oregano

1–1½ tsp dried chilli powder

2 tsp sweet paprika

1 tbs red wine vinegar

2 x 425 g (15 oz) tins kidney beans, drained and rinsed

425 g (15 oz) tin Italian tomatoes

375 ml (13 fl oz/1½ cups) beef stock

1 tbs tomato paste (pureé)

1 dried bay leaf

CORIANDER RICE

250 g (9 oz/1¼ cups) long-grain rice

2–3 tbs chopped coriander (cilantro) leaves

Prep time: 15 minutes + 10 minutes standing

Cooking time: 2 hours

Serves 4

Heat a large, non-stick saucepan or heavy-based casserole dish over a high heat. Cut the pork into 2.5 cm (1 in) cubes. Spray with the oil, then brown the pork in 2 batches for 2–3 minutes, or until evenly browned. Remove the pork. Reduce the heat to medium, spray the pan with the oil, then add the onion and cook for 4–5 minutes, or until soft. Stir in the garlic, cumin, oregano, chilli, paprika and ½ teaspoon salt. Add the vinegar and stir for 30 seconds, or until it evaporates.

Return the pork and any juices to the pan, then add the kidney beans, tomatoes and juice, stock, tomato paste and bay leaf. Stir to combine thoroughly and allow the mixture to come to the boil. Reduce the heat to very low and cook, covered, for 1 hour, stirring frequently.

Remove the lid from the pan and continue to cook, uncovered, for a further 30 minutes, or until the meat is tender and the sauce has reduced and thickened.

Twenty minutes before the pork and bean chilli is ready, rinse the rice and put it in a saucepan. Add 425 ml (15 fl oz/1¾ cups) water and bring to the boil. Cover, reduce the heat to low and cook for 10 minutes. Remove from the heat and leave to stand, covered, for 10 minutes.

Season the pork and bean chilli with salt and black pepper. Stir the coriander through the rice. Place the rice into 4 serving bowls, top with the pork and bean chilli. Garnish with 2 tablespoons chopped flat-leaf (Italian) parsley, 1 tablespoon chopped coriander and 2 teaspoons extra-light sour cream per serve, if you like.

nutrition per serve Energy 2501 kJ (596 Cal); Fat 7.5 g; Carbohydrate 76.1 g; Protein 49 g

lamb koftas in pitta bread

This meal is quick and easy and contains less fat than the take-away version.

500 g (1 lb 2 oz) lean lamb

1 onion, roughly chopped

1 large handful flat-leaf (Italian) parsley, roughly chopped

1 large handful mint, chopped

2 tsp lemon zest

1 tsp ground cumin

¼ tsp chilli powder

250 g (9 oz/1 cup) low-fat yoghurt

2 tsp lemon juice

oil spray

4 wholemeal (wholewheat) pitta breads

TABBOULEH

80 g (3 oz/½ cup) burghul

2 vine-ripened tomatoes

1 Lebanese (short) cucumber

60 g (2¼ oz/½ bunch) flat-leaf (Italian) parsley, chopped

1 large handful mint, chopped

2 French shallots, chopped

125 ml (4 fl oz/½ cup) ready-made fat-free dressing

Prep time: 35 minutes + resting

Cooking time: 15 minutes

Serves 4

Roughly chop the lamb. Put the lamb and onion in a food processor and process until smooth. Add the parsley, mint, lemon zest and spices and process until well combined. Divide the mixture into 24 balls and place on a tray. Cover and refrigerate for at least 30 minutes to allow the flavours to develop.

Meanwhile, to make the tabbouleh, place the burghul in a bowl. Cover with boiling water, set aside for 10 minutes, or until softened. Drain, then use clean hands to squeeze dry. Seed and chop the tomatoes. Cut the cucumber into halves, seed and chop. Place in a large bowl with the parsley, mint, tomatoes, cucumber and shallots. Stir through the fat-free dressing.

To make the yoghurt dressing, combine the yoghurt and lemon juice in a bowl. Cover and refrigerate.

Heat a large, non-stick frying pan and spray with the oil. Cook the lamb balls in 2 batches, spraying with the oil before each batch, until browned all over and cooked through.

Preheat the oven to 180°C (350°F/Gas 4). Cut the pitta pocket breads in half, wrap in foil and place in the oven for 10 minutes.

To serve, divide the tabbouleh between the pitta bread halves, add 3 kofta balls to each and top with the yoghurt dressing.

HINT: Use any flavour of fat-free dressing—Greek, Italian and French all go well with this dish.

nutrition per serve Energy 2401 kJ (572 Cal); Fat 7.9 g; Carbohydrate 73.8 g; Protein 42.3 g

stuffed beef fillet

This nourishing dish shows how easy it is to eat a variety of vegetables in one meal. The meat provides protein as well as iron, zinc and B-group vitamins.

1 tsp olive oil

2 French shallots, finely chopped

60 g (2¼ oz) mushrooms, finely chopped

30 g (1 oz/½ cup) fresh wholemeal (wholewheat) breadcrumbs

1 tbs thyme

1 tbs wholegrain mustard

oil spray

600 g (1 lb 5 oz) lean beef fillet

800 g (1 lb 12 oz) new potatoes, cut into bite-sized chunks

4 corn cobs, each cut in 4 pieces

SAUCE

1 tsp orange zest

185 ml (6 fl oz/¾ cup) orange juice

1 tbs orange marmalade

1 tbs wholegrain mustard

Prep time: 30 minutes

Cooking time: 45 minutes

Serves 4

Preheat the oven to 190°C (375°F/Gas 5). Heat the oil in a non-stick frying pan. Cook the shallots and mushrooms for 2 minutes, or until slightly softened. Place in a small bowl with the breadcrumbs and thyme leaves. Mix in the mustard and 2 teaspoons water to just moisten.

Cut along one side of the fillet to open out or create a butterfly. Spread the mushroom mixture over the surface. Enclose the filling and tie, at intervals, with string. Pat the meat dry with paper towels. Spray a heavy-based frying pan with oil. Heat and add the beef and cook on a high heat until browned all over. Place in a roasting tin. Roast for 25 minutes, or until cooked to your liking. Remove the meat from the oven, cover with foil and rest. Remove the string.

Meanwhile, line a baking tray with baking paper. Place the potatoes in a large saucepan of boiling water. Cook for 5 minutes, or until partially cooked. Drain well. Place the potatoes on the prepared tray. Season with sea salt and spray with oil. Bake for 15–20 minutes, or until crisp and cooked through. Cook the corn cobs in a saucepan of boiling water for 8 minutes, or until tender. Drain.

Add the sauce ingredients to the roasting tin. Stir to dissolve the marmalade and allow it to reduce a little.

To serve, thickly slice the meat. Arrange the meat on plates, drizzle over a little of the sauce and serve with the potatoes and corn.

HINT: If time does not permit, simply roast the whole piece of beef fillet.

nutrition per serve Energy 2113 kJ (503 Cal); Fat 10.7 g; Carbohydrate 56.2 g; Protein 40.8 g

tandoori pork kebabs with rice

The Indian spices blend beautifully with the pork to produce a meal that's rich in flavour. This dish is a good source of protein, potassium and phosphorus.

250 g (9 oz/1 cup) low-fat plain yoghurt

2 cloves garlic, crushed

2 tbs tandoori paste

1 tbs lemon juice

2 tbs chopped coriander (cilantro) leaves

600 g (1 lb 5 oz) lean pork fillet, cubed

1 tsp olive oil

1 onion, chopped

2 cloves garlic, crushed

2 tsp ground cumin

½ tsp paprika

1 tsp ground coriander

375 g (13 oz/2 cups) basmati and wild rice blend

1 litre (35 fl oz/4 cups) vegetable stock

185 g (6¼ oz/¾ cup) low-fat plain yoghurt, extra

1 tbs chopped coriander (cilantro) leaves, extra

Prep time: 20 minutes + 4 hours marinating
Cooking time: 40 minutes
Serves 4

Combine the yoghurt, garlic, tandoori paste, lemon juice and coriander in a large, non-metallic bowl. Add the pork and stir to coat. Refrigerate, covered, for 4 hours.

Heat the oil in a heavy-based saucepan, add the onion, garlic, spices and coriander and cook for 5 minutes, or until golden. Add the rice and stir to coat. Add the stock, bring to the boil, then simmer for 10 minutes, or until tunnels appear in the rice. Reduce the heat to low, cover and cook for 10 minutes.

Thread the pork onto 8 skewers. Heat a chargrill plate and cook for 3–5 minutes on each side, or until tender.

Combine the extra yoghurt and coriander and serve with the pork and spiced rice. Serve with a salad.

HINT: Marinate the pork in the morning before work, then cook when you get home.

nutrition per serve Energy 2765 kJ (658 Cal); Fat 10.7 g; Carbohydrate 86.4 g; Protein 50.4 g

stir-fried thai beef

Apart from the marinating time, this dish is quick to make, and is a good choice for busy people. It contains antioxidants, folate, iron and zinc.

400 g (14 oz) lean sirloin steak, trimmed

2–3 birdseye chillies, seeded and finely chopped

3 cloves garlic, crushed

1 tsp palm sugar or soft brown sugar

2 tbs fish sauce

2 tsp canola oil

400 g (14 oz/2 cups) jasmine rice

150 g (5½ oz) snake beans, sliced into 3 cm (1¼ in) lengths

150 g (5½ oz) sugar snap peas, trimmed

1 large carrot, thinly sliced

1 large handful Thai basil

1–2 birdseye chillies, seeded and finely sliced (optional)

Prep time: 15 minutes + 2 hours marinating

Cooking time: 25 minutes

Serves 4

Slice the meat as thinly as possible, cutting across the grain. Place in a non-metallic bowl with the chilli, garlic, palm sugar, fish sauce and 1 teaspoon of the oil. Toss well to combine, cover and refrigerate for 2 hours.

Thirty minutes before serving, wash the rice well in a sieve until the water runs clear. Put in a saucepan with 750 ml (26 fl oz/3 cups) of water, bring to the boil and boil for 1 minute. Cover, reduce the heat as low as possible and cook for 10 minutes. Turn off the heat and leave the saucepan, covered, for 10 minutes. Fluff the rice with a fork.

Blanch the beans, sugar snap peas and carrot in a large saucepan of boiling water for 2 minutes, drain and refresh. Heat the remaining oil in a large, non-stick wok until very hot and stir-fry the beef in 2 batches over high heat until just browned.

Return all the beef to the wok with the blanched vegetables and basil. Stir-fry for a further 1–2 minutes, or until warmed through. Garnish with sliced chillies, if you like, and serve with the rice.

HINTS: Jasmine rice has a high GI value. For a lower-GI rice, use basmati.

To save time in the evening, you can prepare the meat in the morning and leave it in the fridge to marinate during the day.

nutrition per serve Energy 2501 kJ (596 Cal); Fat 9.5 g; Carbohydrate 91.4 g; Protein 32.9 g

sirloin steaks with roasted capsicum & green olive salad

Full-bodied Mediterranean flavours make these steaks sing. This dish provides good amounts of vitamin C, folate, beta-carotene, potassium, iron and zinc.

1 red capsicum (pepper), seeded and quartered

100 g (3½ oz) green beans, trimmed and halved

750 g (1 lb 10 oz) small new potatoes

500 g (1 lb 2 oz) lean sirloin steak, cut into 4 fillets or 4 x 125 g (4½ oz) fillet steaks

oil spray

250 ml (9 fl oz/1 cup) red wine

2 tbs balsamic vinegar

1 tbs soft brown sugar

10 small thyme leaves

4 handfuls mixed salad

90 g (3¼ oz/½ cup) green olives in brine, pitted and lightly squashed

1 tbs baby capers, drained (optional)

Prep time: 20 minutes
Cooking time: 25 minutes
Serves 4

Preheat a grill (broiler) to medium. Roast the capsicum, skin-side-up, until the skin blackens and blisters. Set aside covered for 5 minutes, then peel away the skin and slice into thin strips. Blanch the beans for 2 minutes in a saucepan of boiling water. Drain and refresh.

Meanwhile, place the potatoes in a saucepan of boiling water. Cook for 12 minutes, or until tender, drain, refresh and halve. Set aside.

Pat the meat dry with paper towels. Spray a non-stick frying pan with the oil and heat to very hot. Add the meat and cook for 2–3 minutes on each side, or until cooked to your liking. Remove from the pan, cover with foil and set aside while preparing the sauce.

Add the wine, vinegar, sugar and half of the thyme leaves to the frying pan. Bring to the boil, stirring continuously. Boil until reduced by about one-third. Set aside until just warm.

Toss together the salad leaves, capsicum and beans in a large bowl. Divide the salad mix equally into 4 large plates or bowls. Scatter over the potatoes, olives and capers, if using. Cut the fillets into 1 cm (½ in) thick slices and arrange on top of the salad. Drizzle over the dressing and garnish with the remaining thyme leaves.

nutrition per serve Energy 1790 kJ (426 Cal); Fat 9 g; Carbohydrate 35.6 g; Protein 32 g

steak with redcurrant jelly

The red wine and redcurrant jelly give the steak exciting flavour. Add the polenta and you have a meal rich in protein, iron, zinc, folate and vitamin K.

4 x 150 g (5½ oz) lean fillet steaks, trimmed

oil spray

1.5 litres (52 fl oz/6 cups) chicken stock

300 g (10¼ oz/2 cups) instant polenta

35 g (1¼ oz/⅓ cup) grated Parmesan

185 ml (6 fl oz/¾ cup) red wine

2 tbs redcurrant jelly

4 spring onions (scallions), chopped

400 g (14 oz) fresh asparagus, trimmed

Prep time: 20 minutes

Cooking time: 25 minutes

Serves 4

Pat the meat dry with a paper towel, then coat liberally with ground black pepper. Spray a large, non-stick frying pan with the oil and cook the meat over a high heat for 2–3 minutes on each side, or until cooked as you like. Remove to a plate, cover with foil and set aside.

Heat the chicken stock in a large saucepan. When it starts to boil, add the polenta in a steady stream, stirring continuously. Lower the heat, stir, and simmer for 5 minutes, or until softened. Stir in the cheese.

Meanwhile, add the wine and jelly to the frying pan. Bring to the boil, stirring to dissolve the jelly. Boil for 5 minutes, or until the sauce is reduced by one-third and becomes a little syrupy. Take care not to burn it. Stir in the spring onions.

While the syrup is reducing, place the asparagus in a steamer. Cover and steam for 2–3 minutes, or until just tender.

To serve, spoon the polenta into the centre of serving plates. Top with the steaks and spoon over the sauce and spring onions. Serve the asparagus on the side.

nutrition per serve Energy 2851 kJ (679 Cal); Fat 16 g; Carbohydrate 70 g; Protein 52.1 g

chilli con carne

This spicy classic provides a sustaining low-GI meal with significant amounts of vitamin C, folate, beta-carotene, B-group vitamins, iron and zinc.

1 tsp canola or olive oil

1 large onion, chopped

1 green capsicum (pepper), seeded and chopped

2 cloves garlic, finely chopped

1 small red chilli, seeded and chopped

1–2 tsp chilli powder

1 tsp ground cumin

500 g (1 lb 2 oz) lean minced (ground) beef

400 g (14 oz) tin chopped tomatoes

1 tbs tomato paste (purée)

1 tbs polenta

400 g (14 oz/2 cups) basmati rice, washed and drained

420 g (14½ oz) tin red kidney beans, drained

1 large handful chopped flat-leaf (Italian) parsley

Prep time: 15 minutes

Cooking time: 50 minutes

Serves 4

Preheat the oven to 180°C (350°F/Gas 4). Heat the canola or olive oil in a large casserole dish. Add the onion, capsicum, garlic and chilli and cook for 3–4 minutes without browning. Stir in the chilli powder and cumin and cook for a further 1 minute.

Increase the heat and add the beef. Cook for 10–12 minutes, stirring, until the beef changes colour and to break up any lumps.

Stir in the tomatoes, tomato paste, 125 ml (4 fl oz/½ cup) water and the polenta. Cover and place in the oven. Bake for 40 minutes.

Meanwhile, bring a pan of water to the boil. Slowly stir in the rice. Bring back to the boil and cook for 12–15 minutes, or until tender. Drain.

Stir the kidney beans and parsley into the mince. Season to taste. Serve hot with the rice and a salad.

nutrition per serve Energy 2790 kJ (644 Cal); Fat 11.3 g; Carbohydrate 97.3 g; Protein 38.7 g

lamb kebabs, raita & couscous

Not only does this meal taste delicious, it is also rich in carbohydrate and protein and is a good source of many vitamins and minerals.

LAMB KEBABS
750 g (1 lb 10 oz) lean lamb
1 tbs Moroccan seasoning
2 tsp lemon juice
2 cloves garlic, crushed
2 small lemons
2 small red onions

RAITA
375 g (13 oz/1½ cups) low-fat plain yoghurt
1 small Lebanese (short) cucumber, peeled, seeded and diced
1 large handful mint, chopped

500 ml (17 fl oz/2 cups) chicken stock
375 g (13 oz/2 cups) couscous
75 g (2½ oz/½ cup) currants
95 g (3¾ oz/½ cup) dried apricots, chopped
35 g (1¼ oz/¼ cup) pistachio nuts, chopped
oil spray

Prep time: 20 minutes + marinating time
Cooking time: 20 minutes
Serves 4

Cut the meat into 3 cm (1¼ in) cubes. Combine the Moroccan seasoning, lemon juice and garlic in a non-metallic bowl, then add the meat. Cover and refrigerate for at least 20 minutes, longer if possible.

To make the raita, combine all the ingredients in a bowl. Set aside.

Heat the stock in a large saucepan. When boiling, turn off the heat and pour in the couscous, stirring continuously. Cover and set aside for 3 minutes to allow the couscous to swell. Return to a low heat and stir with a fork for 2–3 minutes to separate the grains. Stir through the dried fruit and nuts. Set aside.

Preheat the oven grill (broiler) or barbecue grill. Cut each lemon into 8 wedges. Cut each onion into 8 wedges. Thread the lamb, lemon and onion wedges alternately onto 8 x 30 cm (12 in) metal skewers. Spray with the oil and brush with any remaining marinade. Grill (broil) and turn for 10–12 minutes, or until the meat is cooked to your liking. Take care not to overcook or the kebabs will dry out.

Serve the kebabs on a bed of couscous and accompany with the raita. Serve with a mixed green salad.

HINT: Moroccan seasoning is available in supermarkets.

nutrition per serve Energy 3395 kJ (808 Cal); Fat 13.6 g; Carbohydrate 104.7 g; Protein 62.6 g

spiced lamb on dhal with yoghurt

Traditional Eastern spices give this classic Indian dish its wonderful flavour.

3 tsp cumin seeds

1 tbs coriander seeds

1 tsp garam masala

2 x 250 g (9 oz) lamb loin fillets

400 g (14 oz/1¾ cups) rice

oil spray

low-fat plain yoghurt, to serve

DHAL

200 g (7 oz/1 cup) red lentils

¼ tsp ground turmeric

750 ml (26 fl oz/3 cups) chicken stock

2 tsp canola oil

2 tsp brown mustard seeds

2 tsp ground cumin

1 onion, finely chopped

3 cloves garlic, crushed

½ tsp chilli flakes

3 tbs chopped coriander (cilantro) leaves

Prep time: 20 minutes + 2 hours marinating

Cooking time: 1 hour

Serves 4

Place the cumin and coriander seeds and garam masala in a small, dry frying pan and toast for 1 minute, or until fragrant. Put in a spice grinder, or use a mortar and pestle, and grind until coarse. Season with salt and pepper and rub onto the lamb. Cover and refrigerate for 2 hours.

Bring 1 litre (35 fl oz/4 cups) water to the boil in a large saucepan. Stir in the rice. Cover the saucepan, lower the heat and simmer for 20 minutes. Uncover, stir and stand for 5 minutes.

To make the dhal, place the lentils and turmeric in a saucepan, cover with the stock and bring to the boil over high heat. Reduce the heat, simmer for 20 minutes, stirring occasionally, or until the lentils are tender.

Spray a non-stick saucepan with oil, then heat over a high heat. Add the mustard seeds and cumin and cook for 1 minute, or until the mustard seeds begin to pop. Add the onion and cook for 2–3 minutes, or until softened. Add the garlic and chilli and cook for 30 seconds. Add the lentil mixture and coriander, reduce the heat to low and cook for 5 minutes, stirring, or until reduced and thickened. Keep warm.

Lightly spray a chargrill plate with oil and heat over a high heat. Add the lamb and cook for 4–5 minutes on each side. Cover and stand for 5 minutes. Cut into 1cm (½ in) slices on the diagonal.

Divide the rice and dhal onto serving plates and top with the lamb. Put a dollop of yoghurt on top of the lamb or on the side.

HINT: You can serve this dish with traditional raita. See recipe page 196.

nutrition per serve Energy 3175 kJ (756 Cal); Fat 11.7 g; Carbohydrate 108.1 g; Protein 50.5 g

chicken breast with salsa verde

The fresh herbs and vegetables provide not only delicious flavour but also folate and antioxidants to this quick and easy dish.

SALSA VERDE
1 tbs capers in salt
2 cloves garlic, peeled
6 anchovy fillets in brine, drained and rinsed
3 large handfuls flat-leaf (Italian) parsley
1 large handful basil
3 handfuls mint
1 tsp Dijon mustard
1½ tbs red wine vinegar
1 tbs olive oil

750 ml (26 fl oz/3 cups) chicken stock, lightly seasoned
4 x 160 g (5½ oz) skinless chicken breast fillets, without the tenderloin
400 g (14 oz) kipfler potatoes
400 g (14 oz) purple sweet potato, peeled and cut into 5 cm (2 in) pieces
4 large carrots, quartered
2 handfuls rocket (arugula)
2 tsp balsamic vinegar

Prep time: 20 minutes + 10 minutes resting
Cooking time: 25 minutes
Serves 4

Rinse the capers and dry. Chop the capers, garlic and anchovy fillets, and put in the food processor with the parsley, basil and mint, mustard, red wine vinegar and 2 teaspoons water. Process until smooth, then, with the motor running, slowly drizzle in the olive oil until a smooth paste forms. Set aside.

Bring the stock to the boil in a deep frying pan. Add the chicken breasts, bring the stock to a simmer, cover and simmer for 5 minutes. Turn off the heat and allow to sit for 10 minutes. After 10 minutes, the chicken should be cooked through—when touched with your finger, the meat should feel quite springy.

Meanwhile, cook the potatoes and sweet potatoes in a large saucepan of boiling water for 12 minutes, or until tender when pierced with a skewer. Drain. In another saucepan of boiling water, cook the carrots for 6 minutes, or until just tender. Drain.

Place the rocket in a serving bowl, toss with the balsamic vinegar and salt and pepper. Slice the chicken breast and serve with the potatoes, sweet potatoes, carrots and rocket, topped with the salsa verde.

nutrition per serve Energy 2308 kJ (550 Cal); Fat 16.5 g; Carbohydrate 49.3 g; Protein 47.5 g

teriyaki pork with steamed asian greens

This popular Asian dish is alive with an array of intoxicating flavours. It's also a low-fat meal that's rich in beta-carotene, folate and potassium.

500 g (1 lb 2 oz) lean pork fillet

125 ml (4 fl oz/½ cup) dark soy sauce

125 ml (4 fl oz/½ cup) mirin

125 ml (4 fl oz/½ cup) sake

1 tbs grated ginger

2 tsp sugar

400 g (14 oz/2 cups) basmati rice

3 cm x 3 cm (1¼ in x 1¼ in) piece ginger, sliced

300 g (10½ oz) gai larn (Chinese broccoli), cut into 10 cm (4 in) lengths

200 g (7 oz) asparagus, trimmed and cut into 5 cm (2 in) pieces

115 g (4 oz) fresh baby corn, trimmed

1 tsp sesame oil

oil spray

Prep time: 20 minutes + 1 hour marinating

Cooking time: 20 minutes

Serves 4

Thinly slice the pork across the grain. Combine the soy, mirin, sake, ginger and sugar in a large, non-metallic bowl. Add the pork and toss to coat well. Cover and refrigerate for 1 hour.

Bring 1 litre (35 fl oz/4 cups) water to the boil in a large saucepan. Stir in the rice. Cover the saucepan, lower the heat and simmer for 20 minutes. Uncover, stir and stand for 5 minutes.

Meanwhile, fill a wok one-third full of water, and bring to a simmer over a low heat. Line the base of a bamboo steamer with the ginger slices and top with the gai larn, asparagus and corn. Cover with the lid, place over the wok, making sure the water doesn't touch the base and steam for 5–6 minutes, or until the vegetables just cooked. Discard the ginger, drizzle with the sesame oil and season with salt and pepper.

At the same time, lightly spray a non-stick wok with oil and heat over a high heat. Add the pork in two batches and cook for 2–3 minutes, or until cooked. Set aside. Add the marinade and simmer for 4–5 minutes, or until reduced and thickened. Return the pork and stir until warmed through. Serve with the steamed vegetables and rice.

HINTS: Many of the ingredients in this recipe are to be found in Asian food stores or the Asian section of large supermarkets.

You can marinate the pork in the morning and leave in the fridge all day.

nutrition per serve Energy 2593 kJ (617 Cal); Fat 5.8 g; Carbohydrate 90.4 g; Protein 40.3 g

roast chicken with vegetables

Instead of the traditional staple of roast meat and three veg, try this dish of chicken with five different types of vegetables. It has lots of nutrients too.

1.4 kg (3 lb) chicken

1 lemon, halved

6 cloves garlic, unpeeled

6 sprigs thyme

4 potatoes, cut into 5 cm (2 in) pieces

400 g (14 oz) orange sweet potato, peeled and cut into 5 cm (2 in) pieces

400 g (14 oz) butternut pumpkin (squash), peeled and cut into 5 cm (2 in) pieces

oil spray

2 tbs plain (all-purpose) flour

1 tbs Dijon mustard

375 ml (13 fl oz/1½ cups) chicken stock

4 corn cobs, trimmed

400 g (14 oz) green beans, trimmed and halved

Prep time: 30 minutes

Cooking time: 1 hour 10 minutes

Serves 4

Preheat the oven to 200°C (400°F/Gas 6). Season the chicken and place the lemon in the cavity. Bend the wings back and tuck behind the body of the chicken. Tie the drumsticks together using string or skewers. Place the chicken in a large roasting tin and arrange the garlic, thyme and vegetables around it. Spray the chicken and vegetables with the oil, and bake for 1 hour, or until the chicken is tender and the juices run clear. Turn the vegetables after 30 minutes.

Transfer the chicken and vegetables, except the garlic, to separate plates, cover and keep warm. In a large saucepan of boiling water, cook the corn for 8 minutes, then add the beans and cook for a further 2 minutes. Drain.

Meanwhile, pour off any excess fat from the roasting tin. Peel the garlic and mash with a fork in the tin. Heat the tin on the stove top, add the flour and cook over medium heat, stirring, until golden. Remove from the heat and stir in the mustard and stock. Return to the heat and stir until the gravy boils and thickens. Carve the chicken and serve skinless portions of meat with the gravy, roast vegetables, beans and corn.

HINTS: Use two roasting tins if you prefer. Roast the vegetables in one and the chicken in the other.

Microwave or steam the beans and corn, if you prefer.

Make sure you serve the chicken without the skin—that's where most of the fat is.

nutrition per serve Energy 2935 kJ (699 Cal); Fat 19.4 g; Carbohydrate 69.6 g; Protein 53.5 g

steamed chicken on wilted greens

This dish is quick and easy to prepare and provides good amounts of protein, iron, niacin and antioxidants. Serve with rice or noodles to boost the carbohydrate.

DRESSING

2 x 2 cm (¾ x ¾ in) piece ginger, peeled and julienned

125 ml (4 fl oz/½ cup) soy sauce

2 tbs Chinese rice wine

I clove garlic, crushed

½ tsp sesame oil

I tbs finely chopped coriander (cilantro) stems

4 spring onions (scallions), thinly sliced on the diagonal

6 kaffir lime leaves, crushed

I stem lemon grass, cut into thirds and bruised

4 x 4 cm (1½ x 1½ in) piece fresh ginger, sliced

10 g (¼ oz) dried shiitake mushrooms

4 skinless chicken breast fillets

1.6 kg (3 lb 8 oz/2 bunches) gai larn (Chinese broccoli), trimmed and cut into thirds

rice or noodles, to serve

Prep time: 20 minutes
Cooking time: 20 minutes
Serves 4

To make the dressing, place all the ingredients in a bowl and set aside.

Fill a wok one-third full of water. Add the lime leaves, lemon grass, ginger and mushrooms and bring to the boil over a high heat.

Place a large bamboo steamer with a lid over the wok and place the chicken inside. Cover, reduce the heat to a simmer and steam for 10 minutes, or until the chicken is cooked. Remove and keep warm. Add the broccoli to the steamer, cover and steam for 2–3 minutes, or until just wilted. Remove from the heat and keep warm.

Strain the liquid through a sieve, reserving the liquid and the mushrooms. Remove the stems from the mushrooms and thinly slice the caps. Add to the dressing with 125 ml (4 fl oz/½ cup) of the reserved liquid. Cut each chicken breast into 3 pieces on the diagonal.

Divide the gai larn between 4 serving plates, top with the chicken and spoon over the dressing evenly. Serve immediately with noodles or rice.

HINTS: Chinese rice wine (sometimes labelled Shaoxing) is available at Asian food stores. You can replace it with dry sherry.

nutrition per serve Energy 1540 kJ (367 Cal); Fat 11.9 g; Carbohydrate 7.2 g; Protein 50.8 g

pepper beef on potato mash

This steak recipe is low in fat, but rich in flavour and is a good source of protein, iron and zinc. You can add sweet potato to boost the carbohydrate.

6 potatoes

oil spray

6 cloves garlic, unpeeled, ends trimmed

2 tbs whole black peppercorns

½ tsp sea salt

4 x 160 g (5½ oz) lean beef fillet steaks, trimmed

500 g (1 lb 2 oz) broccoli, cut into florets

4 tbs vegetable stock

300 g (10½ oz/½ bunch) baby English spinach leaves

Prep time: 15 minutes

Cooking time: 55 minutes

Serves 4

Preheat the oven to 180°C (350°F/Gas 4). Peel and cut the potatoes into 3 cm (1¼ in) cubes. Spray with oil, and season with salt and pepper. Place on a large baking tray with the garlic cloves, and roast in the oven for 40 minutes, or until golden.

Place the peppercorns in a spice grinder (or use a mortar and pestle) with the sea salt, and roughly crush. Put on a plate, then roll the steaks in the mix until they are well coated.

Over medium heat, heat a chargrill pan, spray with the oil, then add the steaks. Cook for 5 minutes on each side for a medium–rare steak. Remove from the pan and rest, covered, for 2 minutes. Steam or microwave the broccoli for 4 minutes, or until tender.

When the potatoes and garlic are ready, squeeze the garlic from the skin and discard the skin. In a small saucepan, bring the vegetable stock to the boil. Roughly crush the potatoes, garlic and vegetable stock together, using a fork, until softened but still quite chunky.

Place the spinach in a saucepan, cover and place over low–medium heat and cook for 2 minutes, or until the leaves are just beginning to wilt. Remove from the heat, stir and season well.

To serve, divide the mash and broccoli between 4 serving plates, top with the spinach and sit the fillet on top. Drizzle with any of the juices which may have come from the resting steaks.

nutrition per serve Energy 1820 kJ (433 Cal); Fat 10.5 g; Carbohydrate 32.1 g; Protein 44.8 g

beef fillet with red wine sauce & potato purée

Sweet potatoes add colour, fibre and antioxidants to this delicious dish. The lean beef steaks are loaded with protein, iron and zinc.

400 g (14 oz) new potatoes, peeled and cut into 2 cm (¾ in) pieces

400 g (14 oz) orange sweet potato, peeled and cut into 2 cm (¾ in) pieces

6 cloves garlic, peeled

3 tbs beef stock

4 x 150 g (5½ oz) lean beef rib-eye steaks, trimmed

oil spray

150 ml (5 fl oz/⅔ cup) red wine

375 ml (13 fl oz/1½ cups) beef stock

2 tbs tomato paste (purée)

1 tbs soft brown sugar

400 g (14 oz) green beans, trimmed and halved

1 tsp chopped thyme

Prep time: 20 minutes
Cooking time: 35 minutes
Serves 4

Bring a large saucepan of water to the boil and cook the potato, sweet potato and garlic cloves for 10 minutes, or until tender. Drain and mash with a potato masher until smooth. Season with salt and freshly ground black pepper and stir through the stock until smooth.

Meanwhile, season the steaks with freshly ground black pepper on both sides. Spray the oil in a non-stick frying pan and cook the steaks over a medium–high heat for 3–4 minutes on each side, or as you like.

Remove from the pan, cover and keep warm. Add the wine and cook for 1 minute, scraping the base of the pan to loosen any bits. Add the stock, tomato paste and sugar, bring to the boil and cook, stirring occasionally for 8–10 minutes, or until reduced and thickened.

Meanwhile, cook the beans in salted boiling water for 4 minutes.

Stir the thyme into the red wine sauce and season to taste. Spoon over the steaks and serve with the potato purée and green beans.

nutrition per serve Energy 1825 kJ (434 Cal); Fat 10.9 g; Carbohydrate 3.5 g; Protein 39.1 g

Vegetarians must pay particular attention to their diet to ensure they get all of the nutrients that their bodies require. They need to eat a variety of grain products, such as bread, pasta and wholegrain cereals, and legumes, such as lentils, peas and beans, as well as nuts each day to get sufficient protein and carbohydrate, particularly if they don't consume dairy products or eggs.

vegetarian

bean burgers & salad on turkish bread

This carb-rich meal combines ingredients from different food groups to provide a range of amino acids. It also has fibre, folate, potassium and antioxidants.

425 g (15 oz) tin cannellini (white) beans or butter beans, rinsed and drained

oil spray

1 onion, finely chopped

2 cloves garlic, finely chopped

1 green chilli, seeded and finely chopped

1 tsp ground cumin

1 zucchini (courgette), grated

1 carrot, grated

65 g (2½ oz/1 cup) fresh wholegrain breadcrumbs

2 tsp olive oil

1 loaf Turkish pide bread, cut into 4 slices, then sliced horizontally

2 handfuls mixed salad leaves

225 g (8 oz) tin sliced beetroot, drained

2 large ripe tomatoes, sliced

low-fat mayonnaise, to serve

Prep time: 20 minutes + 20 minutes refrigeration
Cooking time: 10 minutes
Serves 4

Mash the beans with a fork and place in a large bowl. Spray a heavy-based frying pan with the oil. Add the onion, garlic and chilli and cook for 3 minutes, or until softened. Stir through the cumin. Transfer the onion mixture to the bowl.

Add the zucchini, carrot and the breadcrumbs. Use clean hands to mix the ingredients. Form into 4 balls, then flatten to 10 cm (4 in) rounds. Cover and refrigerate for at least 20 minutes.

Heat a heavy-based, non-stick frying pan with the olive oil. Cook the burgers over a medium heat for 2–3 minutes on each side, or until golden and heated through. Spray each side with oil as you cook.

To serve, arrange the salad leaves, beetroot and tomato slices on each bun base. Add a bean burger, some mayonnaise, then place the remaining bun half on top.

HINT: You can use other buns or rolls in this recipe.

nutrition per serve Energy 2374 kJ (565 Cal); Fat 11.2 g; Carbohydrate 91.7 g; Protein 21.1 g

red lentil & vegetable lasagne

This wholesome meal is suitable for vegetarians who eat eggs and dairy products. It contains low-GI carbohydrate, complete protein, calcium and antioxidants.

1 tsp vegetable oil
1 onion, chopped
2 cloves garlic, chopped
1 stick celery, diced
1 carrot, diced
1 zucchini (courgette), diced
100 g (3½ oz/½ cup) red lentils
2 x 400 g (15 oz) tins chopped tomatoes
1 tbs tomato paste (purée)
1 tsp sugar
1 tsp dried oregano
500 g (1 lb 2 oz/2 cups) low-fat ricotta
125 ml (4 fl oz/½ cup) skim milk
9 instant lasagne sheets
3 handfuls basil
1 egg, lightly beaten
60 g (2¼ oz/½ cup) low-fat grated Cheddar (we used 50% reduced fat)

Prep time: 25 minutes
Cooking time: 1½ hours
Serves 4–6

Heat the oil in a large, heavy-based saucepan, add the onion and garlic, cook over a low heat for 2 minutes, or until softened. Stir in the celery, carrot and zucchini and cook, stirring, for a further 2 minutes.

Add the lentils, chopped tomatoes, tomato paste, sugar and oregano. Stir in 750 ml (26 fl oz/3 cups) water and bring to the boil. Lower the heat and simmer for 40 minutes, or until the lentils are cooked. Season with salt and pepper and stir frequently.

Preheat the oven to 180°C (350°F/Gas 4). Combine the ricotta and milk in a bowl. Spoon half of the lentil sauce into a 22 x 26 cm (9 x 10 in), 3 litre (105 fl oz/12 cup) ovenproof dish. Top with 3 sheets of lasagne, cutting to fit. Spread over half of the combined ricotta and milk, then scatter over the basil leaves. Top with 3 more pasta sheets. Spread over the remaining half of the lentil sauce, then the remaining 3 sheets of lasagne.

Beat the egg into the remaining half of the ricotta and milk. Spread the surface with the ricotta sauce and sprinkle with the cheese. Bake for 40 minutes. If the top is drying out, sprinkle with water. Serve with salad and bread.

HINT: Freeze any remaining lasagne in portion sizes.

nutrition per serve (6) Energy 1453 kJ (346 Cal); Fat 11.5 g; Carbohydrate 36.3 g; Protein 22.5 g

roast vegetables with chickpeas

High-carb and delicious, this dish, rich in nutrients — fibre, folate, potassium, antioxidants and niacin. Top with yoghurt to add calcium and other minerals.

500 g (1 lb 2 oz) sweet potato, peeled and cut into 1.5 cm (½ in) thick slices on the diagonal

3 x 185 g (6¼ oz) baby eggplant (aubergine), cut into 2 cm (¾ in) thick slices on the diagonal

2 sprigs rosemary, leaves chopped

oil spray

2 zucchini (courgettes), each cut into 4 batons

1 red capsicum (pepper), seeded and cut into thick slices

1 large red onion, cut into 8 wedges

3 ripe Roma (plum) tomatoes, quartered

2 tbs balsamic vinegar

375 ml (13 fl oz/1½ cups) chicken stock

280 g (10 oz/1½ cups) couscous

425 g (15 oz) tin chickpeas, rinsed and drained

1 handful mixed herbs (chives, basil, parsley), chopped

Prep time: 15 minutes
Cooking time: 55 minutes
Serves 4

Preheat the oven to 180°C (350°F/Gas 4). Line a large baking tray with baking paper or use 2 smaller trays. Place the sweet potato and eggplant on the prepared tray. Add the rosemary. Spray with the oil and use clean hands to toss the vegetables to coat with the oil. Arrange in a single layer. Bake for 15 minutes.

Toss through the zucchinis, capsicum and onion. Spray again with the oil. Bake for a further 15 minutes.

Add the tomato wedges, drizzle with balsamic vinegar (or use balsamic spray) and bake for 15 minutes, or until all the vegetables are tender.

Meanwhile, heat the stock in a saucepan. When boiling, turn off the heat and pour in the couscous, stirring continuously. Cover and set aside for 3 minutes to allow the couscous to swell. Return to a low heat and stir with a fork for 2–3 minutes to separate the grains. Add the chickpeas and most of the herbs. Serve the vegetables on warm couscous (or at room temperature). Garnish with the extra herbs.

nutrition per serve Energy 2208 kJ (526 Cal); Fat 4.6 g; Carbohydrate 92.7 g; Protein 21.8 g

green lentil & vegetable curry

If you like a little spice in your meals this one's perfect. It also contains a range of healthy plant food compounds. Serve with rice for extra carbohydrate.

1 tsp canola oil

1 large onion, chopped

2 cloves garlic, chopped

1–2 tbs curry paste

1 tsp ground turmeric

200 g (7 oz/1 cup) green lentils, rinsed and drained

1.25 litres (44 fl oz/5 cups) vegetable stock or water

1 large carrot, cut into 2 cm (¾ in) cubes

2 potatoes, cut into 2 cm (¾ in) cubes

250 g (9 oz) sweet potato, peeled and cut into 2 cm (¾ in) cubes

350 g (12 oz) cauliflower, broken into small florets

150 g (5½ oz) green beans, trimmed and halved

basil, to serve

coriander (cilantro) leaves, to serve

Prep time: 20 minutes

Cooking time: 1 hour 5 minutes

Serves 4

Heat the oil in a saucepan over a medium heat. Add the onion and garlic and cook for 3 minutes, or until softened. Stir in the curry paste and turmeric and stir for 1 minute. Add the lentils and stock or water.

Bring to the boil, then reduce the heat. Cover and simmer for 30 minutes, then add the carrot, potatoes and sweet potato. Simmer, covered, for 20 minutes, or until the lentils and vegetables are tender.

Add the cauliflower and beans, cover and simmer for 10 minutes, or until the cauliflower and beans are cooked and most of the liquid has been absorbed. Remove the lid and simmer for a further few minutes if there is too much liquid. Serve hot with brown or basmati rice and top with basil and coriander leaves.

nutrition per serve Energy 1390 kJ (331 Cal); Fat 6 g; Carbohydrate 43.5 g; Protein 20.1 g

spanakopita with tomato salad

This reduced-fat version of the traditional Greek favourite is deliciously cheesy. It is also a good source of folate, magnesium, calcium and phosphorus.

1 kg (2 lb 4 oz/1 bunch) silverbeet (Swiss chard)

oil spray

1 onion, chopped

125 g (4½ oz) spring onions (scallions), chopped

125 g (4½ oz) low-fat fetta

250 g (9 oz/1 cup) low-fat creamed cottage cheese

30 g (1 oz) pecorino, grated

1 tsp chopped dill

¼ tsp ground nutmeg

2 eggs, lightly beaten

8 sheets filo pastry

TOMATO SALAD

8 ripe Roma (plum) tomatoes

3 French shallots, thinly sliced

1 tbs finely chopped oregano

2 tbs ready-made fat-free Greek dressing

Prep time: 30 minutes

Cooking time: 1 hour

Serves 4

Preheat the oven to 180°C (350°F/Gas 4). Rinse the silverbeet and remove thick stems. Blanch the leaves in a saucepan of salted boiling water for 3–4 minutes, or until tender. Remove with a slotted spoon and drain in a colander. When slightly cool, wrap in a cloth and twist the ends to remove excess moisture. Roughly chop and set aside.

Heat a non-stick pan and spray with the oil. Add the onion and cook over a medium heat for 6–7 minutes, or until softened. Add the spring onions and cook for 2 minutes, then add the silverbeet, combining well. Remove from the heat and allow to cool to room temperature.

Spray a 2.5 litre (87 fl oz/10 cup), 20 × 25 cm (8 × 10 in) baking dish with oil. Put the cheeses in a bowl, add the silverbeet mixture, dill and nutmeg. Add the eggs and season with salt and ground black pepper.

Line the base and sides of the baking dish with a sheet of filo pastry. Spray with the oil and cover with another sheet of filo. Repeat until 4 sheets of pastry have been used. Spoon in the filling. Fold any exposed pastry up and over to cover the top of the filling. Cover with a sheet of pastry, spray lightly with the oil and continue until all the sheets of filo are used. Trim the pastry with scissors, then tuck the excess inside the dish. Spray the top with oil. Use a knife to score the surface into diamonds. Bake for 45 minutes, or until the pastry is puffed and golden. Leave to rest at room temperature for 10 minutes.

Meanwhile, prepare the tomato salad by tossing all the ingredients in a bowl; season to taste with salt and freshly ground black pepper. Serve with the spanakopita.

nutrition per serve Energy 1459 kJ (347 Cal); Fat 12.3 g; Carbohydrate 25.9 g; Protein 30.1 g

chilli beans with polenta

Suitable for vegetarians who eat dairy products, this delightfully spicy dish is rich in fibre and provides complete protein plus good amounts of antioxidants.

420 g (14½ oz) tin creamed corn

375 ml (13 fl oz/1½ cups) vegetable stock

70 g (2½ oz/½ cup) instant polenta

310 g (10½ oz) tin corn kernels, drained

40 g (1½ oz/⅓ cup) low-fat vintage Cheddar, grated

1 tbs chopped coriander (cilantro) leaves

1 tbs olive oil

1 red onion, sliced

2 cloves garlic, crushed

1 tsp chilli powder

1 tsp paprika

1 tbs ground cumin

1 tsp ground coriander

400 g (14 oz) tin kidney beans, rinsed and drained

400 g (14 oz) tin borlotti beans, rinsed and drained

800 g (1 lb 12 oz) tin tomatoes

2 tbs tomato paste (pureé)

2 tbs chopped coriander (cilantro) leaves

Prep time: 15 minutes

Cooking time: 35 minutes

Serves 6

Line a 20 cm (8 in) round cake tin with plastic wrap. Place the creamed corn and stock in a saucepan and bring to the boil. Stir in the polenta and corn kernels, and cook over a medium heat until it comes away from the sides. Stir in the cheese and coriander, cool for 5 minutes, then spoon into the tin and level the surface. Cool.

Heat the oil in a large saucepan, add the onion, garlic and spices and cook until soft. Stir in the beans, tomato and tomato paste. Simmer for 20 minutes. Stir in the coriander.

Lift the polenta from the tin with the aid of the plastic wrap, cut into wedges and serve with the chilli beans and a salad on the side.

nutrition per serve Energy 1402 kJ (334 Cal); Fat 6.9 g; Carbohydrate 49.8 g; Protein 14.2 g

tofu with greens & noodles

If you think tofu is bland, wait till you've tried this dish. When marinated, the tofu soaks up all the flavours. This dish has antioxidants, fibre and iron.

MARINADE

3 tbs vegetarian oyster sauce

3 tbs hoisin sauce

2 tbs reduced-salt soy sauce

1½ tbs soft brown sugar

3 tsp grated ginger

3 cloves garlic, crushed

300 g (10½ oz) firm tofu, drained and cut into 2 cm (¾ in) cubes

300 g (10½ oz) dried thin egg noodles

1 tsp canola oil

4 Asian shallots, thinly sliced

1 small red capsicum (pepper), seeded and thinly sliced

200 g (7 oz) sugar snap peas, trimmed

400 g (14 oz) broccolini, cut into 5 cm (2 in) lengths

125 ml (4 fl oz/½ cup) vegetable stock or water

coriander (cilantro) leaves, to serve

Prep time: 15 minutes + 30 minutes marinating

Cooking time: 15 minutes

Serves 4

Combine the marinade ingredients in a non-metallic bowl, add the tofu and gently stir through. Cover and refrigerate for at least 30 minutes, longer if possible.

Cook the noodles according to the manufacturer's directions and drain. Cut the noodles into shorter lengths using scissors.

Heat the oil in a large wok. Add the shallots and capsicum and stir-fry for 2 minutes, or until slightly softened. Add the peas, broccolini and stock. Cover and cook for 2–3 minutes, or until the vegetables are just tender, stirring occasionally.

Add the tofu with the marinade ingredients and the noodles. Gently combine and stir until heated through. Serve immediately garnished with the coriander leaves.

HINT: Use broccoli florets if broccolini is not available.

nutrition per serve Energy 2121 kJ (505 Cal); Fat 9 g; Carbohydrate 73 g; Protein 26.9 g

vegetable tagine

This low-fat, Moroccan-style dish has a wonderful spicy flavour. It also contains loads of carbohydrate, fibre, folate, antioxidants and potassium.

1.5 kg (3 lb 5 oz) mixed vegetables

1 tbs olive oil

2 onions, chopped

1 tsp ground ginger

2 tsp paprika

2 tsp ground cumin

1 cinnamon stick

pinch saffron threads

½ preserved lemon, rinsed, flesh and pith removed, thinly sliced

400 g (14 oz) tin chopped tomatoes

250 ml (9 oz/1 cup) vegetable stock

100 g (3½ oz) dried pears, halved

55 g (2 oz/¼ cup) pitted prunes

2 zucchini (courgettes), cut into large chunks

300 g (10½ oz/1⅔ cups) instant couscous

1 tsp grated orange zest

3 tbs chopped flat-leaf (Italian) parsley

Prep time: 20 minutes

Cooking time: 1 hour

Serves 4–6

Preheat the oven to moderate 180°C (350°F/Gas 4). Peel, then cut the vegetables (see Hints, below, for choices) into large chunks. Heat the oil in a large casserole dish, add the onion and spices, and cook for 5 minutes, or until soft.

Add the vegetables and cook, stirring, for 5 minutes, or until soft. Add the preserved lemon, tomato, stock, dried pears and prunes. Cover, and bake for 30 minutes. Add the zucchinis and cook for 15 minutes, or until tender.

Cover the couscous with 500 ml (17 fl oz/2 cups) boiling water, stir in the zest and leave until the water is absorbed. Stir with a fork. Stir the parsley through the vegetables. Serve the vegetables on a bed of couscous.

HINTS: Carrot, eggplant (aubergine), potato and pumpkin all work well in this dish.

Preserved lemon is available from delicatessens. Use 2 teaspoons grated lemon zest if not available.

nutrition per serve Energy 1793 kJ (427 Cal); Fat 4.8 g; Carbohydrate 77.7 g; Protein 13.6 g

tofu burger with vegetables

This hearty burger is not only very filling but it also packs a healthy punch with fibre, carbohydrate, folate, vitamin C, inorganic iron and calcium.

15 g (½ oz) porcini mushrooms

2 red capsicums (peppers)

oil spray

2 red onions, finely chopped

6 cloves garlic, crushed

400 g (14 oz) Swiss brown mushrooms, finely chopped

1 small handful basil, shredded

3 tbs finely chopped flat-leaf (Italian) parsley

2 tbs finely chopped oregano

3 tbs red wine

3 tbs vegetable stock

500 g (1 lb 2 oz) hard tofu

200 g (7 oz/2½ cups) fresh breadcrumbs

1 egg, lightly beaten

750 g (1 lb 10 oz) kipfler potatoes, cut into 2 cm (¾ in) slices on the diagonal

4 round wholegrain rolls

2 handfuls baby rocket (arugula) leaves

160 g (5¾ oz/⅔ cup) ready-made tomato relish

Prep time: 25 minutes + 2 hours refrigeration

Cooking time: 1¼ hours

Serves 4

Preheat the oven to 200°C (400°F/Gas 6). Put the porcini mushrooms in a bowl, pour over boiling water to cover and stand for 20 minutes. Drain. Squeeze out excess moisture and finely chop.

Seed and quarter the capsicums. Put under a preheated grill (broiler), skin-side-up, and grill (broil) for 10 minutes, or until the skin blackens and blisters. Put in a plastic bag to cool, then peel off the skin.

Spray a non-stick pan with oil over a high heat and cook the onion for 2–3 minutes, or until softened. Add the garlic, Swiss brown and porcini mushrooms and cook for 2–3 minutes, or until softened. Stir through the herbs, then add the wine and boil for 1 minute. Add the stock and cook, stirring for 4–5 minutes, or until the liquid has evaporated. Cool. Finely grate the tofu. Transfer to a bowl and stir through the tofu, 40 g (1½ oz/½ cup) of the breadcrumbs and egg until combined. Season with salt and pepper. Refrigerate for 2 hours.

Meanwhile, place the potatoes in a baking dish and spray with the oil, tossing to coat. Sprinkle with sea salt and bake for 45 minutes, turning halfway through, or until golden.

Divide the tofu mixture into 4 patties and coat in the remaining breadcrumbs. Spray a non-stick pan with oil and heat over a high heat. Cook the patties for 4–5 minutes on each side, or until golden.

Halve the rolls and toast. Divide the rocket between each of the bottom halves, then add a patty. Add the capsicum and top with relish. Season. Cover with the lid and serve with the potatoes.

nutrition per serve Energy 3119 kJ (743 Cal); Fat 16.2 g; Carbohydrate 97.8 g; Protein 39.8 g

vegetable stir-fry
with egg noodles

This tasty light meal, with its distinctive Asian flavours, is quick and easy to make. It's also rich in various antioxidants, folate and potassium.

200 g (7 oz) dried egg noodles

2 tsp canola oil

8 spring onions (scallions), cut into 2.5 cm (1 in) lengths

3 x 3 cm (1¼ x 1¼ in) piece fresh ginger, julienned

2 cloves garlic, crushed

200 g (7 oz) Swiss brown mushrooms, quartered

1 red capsicum (pepper), seeded and thinly sliced

1 zucchini (courgette), cut on the diagonal into 1 cm (½ in) slices

1 carrot, sliced on the diagonal

300 g (10½ oz) broccoli, cut into small florets

300 g (10½ oz) Chinese cabbage, shredded

2 tbs hoisin sauce

3 tbs sake or dry sherry

1 handful coriander (cilantro) leaves, plus extra, to serve

300 g (10½ oz) packet firm tofu, drained and cut into cubes

Prep time: 20 minutes

Cooking time: 15 minutes

Serves 4

Bring a large saucepan of water to the boil. Add the noodles and cook for 5 minutes or until tender. Drain.

Heat a wok over a high heat, add the canola oil and swirl to coat. Add the spring onions and ginger and stir-fry for 1 minute. Add the garlic and mushrooms and cook for 1 minute.

Add the capsicum, zucchini, carrot and broccoli to the wok and stir-fry for 3–4 minutes. Add 1–2 tablespoons water to help steam through, if necessary. Add the cabbage, hoisin sauce and sake and stir-fry for 2–3 minutes, or until the cabbage has wilted and all ingredients are well combined.

Toss through the tofu, noodles and coriander until well coated in the sauce and serve immediately. Serve with coriander leaves.

nutrition per serve Energy 1726 kJ (411 Cal); Fat 10.4 g; Carbohydrate 47 g; Protein 23 g

The recipes in this section have been designed to help you indulge your sweet tooth without consuming too much fat or excessive kilojoules. Low-fat ingredients can be used to make healthier versions of traditional desserts, and fruit can add flavour, antioxidants and carbohydrate. Healthy desserts can be quickly prepared if you have low-fat dairy products and baking mixes and some fruit stocked in the pantry or the fridge.

sweets

spiced apple, blueberry & bran muffins

Light and low in fat, these moist fruity muffins are ideal snacks to take with you to sporting events or training. The hint of cinnamon works a treat.

155 g (5½ oz/1¼ cups) self-raising flour

110 g (3¾ oz/¾ cup) wholemeal (wholewheat) self-raising flour

1 tsp ground cinnamon

80 g (2¾ oz/½ cup) unprocessed oat bran

140 g (5 oz/¾ cup) soft brown sugar

150 g (5½ oz/1 cup) fresh or frozen blueberries

140 g (5 oz/½ cup) ready-made chunky apple sauce

1 egg, lightly beaten

250 ml (9 fl oz/1 cup) skim milk

2 egg whites

Prep time: 20 minutes + cooling
Cooking time: 20 minutes
Makes 12

Preheat the oven to 200°C (400°F/Gas 6). Sift the flours and cinnamon into a large bowl and return the husks from the wholemeal flour to the bowl. Stir in the oat bran, sugar and blueberries.

Place the apple sauce, egg, milk and egg whites in a jug and mix together well. Pour into the dry ingredients and mix until just combined, but still lumpy. Do not overmix.

Spoon the mixture into twelve 125 ml (4 fl oz/½ cup) non-stick muffin holes and bake for 20 minutes, or until cooked through. Stand for 5 minutes in the tin before turning out on a wire rack to cool.

nutrition per muffin Energy 720 kJ (171 Cal); Fat 1.2 g; Carbohydrate 33.9 g; Protein 5.4 g

health fruit bars

These bars have a high GI value, and so can be useful as a recovery snack after training or events, particularly if you're exercising again on the same day.

60 g (2¼ oz/2 cups) puffed rice breakfast cereal

150 g (5½ oz/1½ cups) raw rolled oats

30 g (1 oz/¼ cup) sunflower seeds

40 g (1½ oz/¼ cup) sesame seeds

200 g (7 oz) dried fruit medley

60 g (2¼ oz/⅓ cup) rice flour

125 ml (4 fl oz/½ cup) glucose syrup

90 g (3¼ oz/¼ cup) honey

Prep time: 10 minutes + cooling

Cooking time: 20 minutes

Makes 16–20

Preheat the oven to 180°C (350°F/Gas 4). Line the base and 2 long sides of a 29 x 19 cm (11½ x 7½ in) baking tin with baking paper. Place the puffed rice cereal, rolled oats, sunflower seeds, sesame seeds, dried fruit and rice flour in a bowl, and mix together well.

Place the glucose and honey in a small saucepan, and heat gently over a medium heat for 2 minutes, or until runny. Stir the syrup into the dry ingredients and mix well to coat.

Press the mixture firmly into the prepared tin. Place a sheet of baking paper over the mixture and use the back of a spoon or a measuring cup to spread evenly. Remove the top sheet of baking paper. Bake for 20 minutes, or until golden brown. Leave to cool and crisp in the tin before lifting out and cutting into fingers. Store in an airtight container in the refrigerator.

HINTS: Glucose syrup and rice flour are available from large supermarkets and health-food shops.

Any low-fat sports breakfast cereal can be used in this recipe in place of the puffed rice.

nutrition per bar (20) Energy 578 kJ (138 Cal); Fat 2.7 g; Carbohydrate 25.6 g; Protein 2.3 g

apricot & fig bran bread

This delicious fruity bread is low in fat and makes an excellent light meal or snack. It also provides good amounts of fibre and carbohydrate.

oil spray

110 g (3¾ oz/1 cup) unprocessed oat bran

250 ml (9 fl oz/1 cup) skim or no-fat milk

80 g (2¾ oz/½ cup) dried apricots, quartered

110 g (3¾ oz/½ cup dried figs, quartered

185 g (6¼ oz/1 cup) soft brown sugar

150 g (5½ oz/1 cup) self-raising flour

1 tsp ground cinnamon

Prep time: 15 minutes + 10 minutes soaking time

Cooking time: 45 minutes

Makes 1 loaf (10–12 slices)

Preheat the oven to 180°C (350°F/Gas 4). Spray a 10 x 18 cm (4 x 7 in) loaf tin with the oil and line the base with baking paper.

Put the bran in a large bowl. Stir in the milk, dried fruit and sugar. Set aside for 10 minutes to soften the bran.

Meanwhile, sift the flour and cinnamon into a bowl. Stir the combined flour and cinnamon into the bran mixture. Pour into the prepared tin and bake for 45 minutes, or until cooked when a skewer inserted into the centre of the loaf comes out clean. Cool in the tin for 10 minutes, then turn out. Cut into thick slices to serve.

HINT: Leftovers of this loaf are delicious when toasted. You can freeze the loaf for up to 1 month. Use any 2–3 varieties of dried fruit or fruit medley in this recipe.

nutrition per slice (12) Energy 752 kJ (179 Cal); Fat 4.2 g; Carbohydrate 37.5 g; Protein 4.2 g

carrot cake with ricotta topping

This reduced-fat version of carrot cake is just as tasty as the regular kind and contains more fibre. It is also a good source of the antioxidant, beta-carotene.

310 g (10¾ oz/2½ cups) self-raising flour

1 tsp bicarbonate of soda

2 tsp ground cinnamon

1 tsp mixed spice

90 g (3¼ oz/½ cup) soft brown sugar

60 g (2¼ oz/½ cup) sultanas

2 eggs, lightly beaten

2 tbs canola oil

4 tbs skim or no-fat milk

140 g (5 oz/½ cup) apple purée

300 g (10½ oz) carrots, coarsely grated

125 g (4½ oz/½ cup) ricotta

30 g (1 oz/¼ cup) icing (confectioner's) sugar

1 tsp lime zest

Prep time: 20 minutes

Cooking time: 1¼ hours

Makes 14 slices

Preheat the oven to 180°C (350°F/Gas 4). Lightly grease a 10 x 18 cm (4 x 7 in) loaf tin and line the base with baking paper.

Sift the flour, soda and spices into a large bowl. Stir in the brown sugar and sultanas. Combine the eggs, oil, milk and apple purée in a large jug.

Stir the egg mixture into the flour mixture, then stir in the carrot. Spread into the prepared tin and bake for 1¼ hours, or until a skewer comes out clean and the cake comes away slightly from the sides. Leave for 5 minutes, then turn out onto a wire rack.

Beat the ricotta, icing sugar and zest together until smooth. Spread over the cooled cake.

nutrition per slice Energy 773 kJ (184 Cal); Fat 4.8 g; Carbohydrate 30.3 g; Protein 4.6 g

wholemeal banana bread

This filling bread is rich in carbohydrate and also provides some omega-3 fatty acids. Serve with yoghurt to boost your intake of calcium and other minerals.

oil spray

90 g (3¼ oz/½ cup) soft brown sugar

1 egg

250 g (9 oz/1 cup) low-fat vanilla fromage frais

2 tbs canola oil

235 g (8½ oz/1 cup) mashed banana

30 g (1 oz/¼ cup) sultanas

125 g (4½ oz/1 cup) self-raising flour

50 g (1¾ oz/¼ cup) wholemeal (wholewheat) self-raising flour

½ tsp bicarbonate of soda

2 tbs unprocessed wheatbran

1 tsp ground cinnamon

½ tsp ground nutmeg

low-fat plain yoghurt or fromage frais, to serve

Prep time: 15 minutes
Cooking time: 50 minutes
Serves 4–6

Preheat the oven to 160°C (315°F/Gas 2–3). Spray a 10 x 18 cm (4 x 7 in) loaf tin with canola oil and line the base with baking paper.

Put the brown sugar, egg, fromage frais and oil in a large bowl and whisk until well combined. Stir in the bananas and sultanas, then fold in the sifted flours, bicarbonate of soda, bran, cinnamon and nutmeg. Return the husks to the bowl.

Spoon the mixture into the prepared tin and bake in the oven for 50 minutes, or until cooked through when tested with a skewer. Serve warm or cold with low-fat yoghurt or fromage frais. It is also delicious toasted.

HINT: Two ripe bananas will yield 1 cup mashed banana.

nutrition per serve (6) Energy 1251 kJ (298 Cal); Fat 7.8 g; Carbohydrate 51.9 g; Protein 8.7 g

reduced-fat fudge brownies

Great as a dessert or snack, these brownies show that reduced-fat foods can be delicious too. For a dessert, serve with fromage frais to add extra nutrients.

oil spray

60 g (2¼ oz/½ cup) plain (all-purpose) flour

60 g (2¼ oz/½ cup) self-raising flour

1 tsp bicarbonate of soda

90 g (3¼ oz/¾ cup) cocoa powder

2 eggs

285 g (10 oz/1¼ cups) caster (superfine) sugar

2 tsp vanilla essence

2 tbs canola oil

200 g (7 oz) low-fat vanilla fromage frais or vanilla yoghurt

140 g (5 oz/½ cup) apple purée

icing (confectioner's) sugar, for dusting

Prep time: 15 minutes
Cooking time: 30 minutes
Makes 18

Preheat the oven to 180°C (350°F/Gas 4). Spray a 30 × 20 cm (12 × 8 in) shallow baking tin with the oil and line the base and 2 long sides with baking paper.

Sift the flours, bicarbonate of soda and cocoa powder into a large bowl. Combine the eggs, sugar, vanilla essence, oil, fromage frais or yoghurt and apple purée. Add to the flour and mix well. Spread into the tin and bake for 30 minutes, or until a skewer comes out clean.

The brownie will sink slightly in the centre as it cools. Leave in the tin for 5 minutes before turning onto a wire rack to cool. Dust with icing sugar, cut into pieces and serve.

nutrition per brownie Energy 611 kJ (145 Cal); Fat 3.5 g; Carbohydrate 25.3 g; Protein 3.3 g

strawberry & banana ice

This dessert is a delicious alternative to ice cream and suitable for people who are intolerant to dairy foods. It provides antioxidants, fibre and most minerals.

300 g (10½ oz) silken tofu, chopped

250 g (9 oz/1⅓ cups) strawberries, roughly chopped

2 ripe bananas, roughly chopped

55 g (2 oz/¼ cup) caster (superfine) sugar

Prep time: 15 minutes + freezing

Cooking time: Nil

Serves 4

Place the tofu, strawberries, bananas and caster sugar in a blender or food processor and process until smooth.

Pour the mixture into a shallow cake tin and freeze for 3 hours, or until almost frozen. Break up roughly with a fork or a spoon, then transfer to a large bowl and beat until it has a smooth texture. Pour the mixture evenly into a suitable container, cover and freeze again, until quite firm.

Alternatively, freeze the blended mixture in an ice cream machine according to the manufacturer's instructions, until thick and creamy, then store in a covered container in the freezer.

Transfer to the refrigerator for about 30 minutes before serving to allow the ice to soften slightly. Scoop the ice into bowls to serve.

HINT: Silken tofu is readily available in the refrigerated section of most supermarkets and health-food shops. You can also buy it in long-life packets. Make sure you buy silken tofu as this type does not go lumpy.

nutrition per serve Energy 859 kJ (204 Cal); Fat 5.2 g; Carbohydrate 27.7 g; Protein 10.8 g

poached pears in vanilla syrup

Pears have never tasted so good! They're also easily digested and provide potassium and fibre. Top with yoghurt to add calcium and other minerals.

170 g (6 oz/¾ cup) caster (superfine) sugar

1 vanilla bean, split in half and scraped

1 strip lemon zest

1½ tsp lemon grass tea leaves

4 large firm pears, peeled with stems intact

100 g (3½ oz/⅓ cup) low-fat plain yoghurt, to serve

Prep time: 15 minutes

Cooking time: 50 minutes

Serves 4

Put the sugar, vanilla bean and lemon zest in a large saucepan with 500 ml (17 fl oz/2 cups) water. Put the lemon grass in a tea-infuser ball or small muslin bag, and add to the saucepan. Heat over a low heat, stirring occasionally, until the sugar melts.

Bring to the boil, then reduce to a simmer and add the pears, laying them on their sides. Cover and simmer, turning occasionally, for 30 minutes, or until the pears are tender when pierced with a skewer.

Remove the pears with a slotted spoon and set aside to cool. Meanwhile, increase the heat to high and simmer the syrup for 8–10 minutes, or until reduced by half and thickened slightly. Remove the vanilla bean, lemon zest and lemon grass tea. Serve the pears drizzled with the syrup and a dollop of the yoghurt on the side.

HINT: If you place the lemon grass tea in a tea-infuser ball or muslin bag, it can readily be removed, as it is too fine to be strained from the syrup.

nutrition per serve Energy 1224 kJ (291 Cal); Fat 0.3 g; Carbohydrate 71 g; Protein 2.4 g

yoghurt & savoiardi parfait

Most of the fat in this dessert is monounsaturated and comes from the almonds. The berries and passionfruit provide fibre, vitamin C and antioxidants.

750 g (1 lb 10 oz/3 cups) low-fat plain yoghurt

55 g (2 oz/¼ cup) sugar

strained juice from 12 passionfruit

125 g (4½ oz) savoiardi (sponge finger biscuits), cut to fit parfait glasses

500 g (1 lb 2 oz/3 cups) fresh or frozen raspberries

40 g (1½ oz/⅓ cup) slivered almonds, toasted

Prep time: 20 minutes + 1 hour refrigeration

Cooking time: Nil

Serves 6

Place the yoghurt, sugar and passionfruit juice in a bowl and mix well to combine. Divide one-third of the mixture among six 250 ml (9 fl oz/1 cup) parfait glasses.

Top the yoghurt mixture with a layer of savoiardi biscuits, then with a layer of raspberries.

Repeat with another layer of yoghurt, biscuits and raspberries, and top with a layer of yoghurt. Top with the remaining raspberries and the toasted almonds. Refrigerate for 1 hour before serving.

HINT: You can use strawberries instead of raspberries, if you prefer. Hull and slice the strawberries, before using.

nutrition per serve Energy 1551 kJ (369 Cal); Fat 7.7 g; Carbohydrate 37.8 g; Protein 18.2 g

tangy lime delicious

This yummy dessert is rich in carbohydrate and is perfect for cold winter nights. Top with a low-fat dairy product, such as ice cream to add extra minerals.

30 g (1 oz) butter
250 g (9 oz/1 cup) sugar
1 tbs lime zest
2 eggs, separated
40 g (1½ oz/⅓ cup) self-raising flour
150 ml (5 fl oz) skim milk
125 ml (4 fl oz/½ cup) lime juice

Prep time: 20 minutes
Cooking time: 40 minutes
Serves 4–6

Preheat the oven to 180°C (350°F/Gas 4). Lightly grease a 1 litre (35 fl oz/4 cup) ovenproof dish.

Beat the butter, sugar and lime zest together until light and creamy. Gradually add the egg yolks, beating well between each addition.

Fold in the flour, milk and lime juice alternately. Place the egg whites in a clean, dry bowl and beat until soft peaks form. Fold into the butter and sugar mixture, then pour into the prepared dish and bake for 40 minutes, or until golden. Serve with low-fat ice cream, if you like.

nutrition per serve (6) Energy 1079 kJ (257 Cal); Fat 5.9 g; Carbohydrate 48.4 g; Protein 3.9 g

orange & bread pudding

A low-fat alternative to bread and butter pudding, this lovely tangy version is a good source of carbohydrate and provides most vitamins and minerals.

1 loaf day-old wholemeal (wholewheat) bread

60 g (2¼ oz/½ cup) raisins

2 eggs

1 egg white

115 g (4 oz/½ cup) caster (superfine) sugar, plus ½ tsp

2 tsp vanilla essence

500 ml (17 fl oz/2 cups) skim milk

1 tsp finely chopped orange zest

2 tbs orange marmalade

½ tsp ground cinnamon

Prep time: 15 minutes
Cooking time: 55 minutes
Serves 6–8

Preheat the oven to 180°C (350°F/Gas 4). You will need a 2 litre (75 fl oz /8 cup) square or oval ovenproof dish with a depth of at least 5 cm (2 in).

Cut the bread into sufficient slices to make 2 layers in the pudding dish. Remove the crusts. Cover the bottom of the pudding dish with 1 layer of bread. Scatter with two-thirds of the raisins.

Whisk the eggs, egg white, sugar and vanilla in a large bowl until light and frothy, then add the milk and orange zest. Pour half the mixture into the dish and top with another layer of bread. Put the marmalade in a small saucepan with 1 teaspoon water and heat over a low heat until melted. Lightly brush the mixture over the bread and scatter on the remaining raisins. Pour the remaining egg mixture into the dish, a little at a time so the bread can absorb it. Mix the extra caster sugar with the cinnamon, then lightly sprinkle the mixture over the top of the bread.

Place the dish in a larger baking dish and pour in enough boiling water to come halfway up the sides of the pudding dish. Bake for 55 minutes, or until just set. Serve warm.

nutrition per serve (8) Energy 1066 kJ (254 Cal); Fat 2.9 g; Carbohydrate 47.1 g; Protein 9.4 g

apple & strawberry crumble

This dessert delivers everything you want in a crumble with less fat and kilojoules than traditional fruit crumbles. It is also rich in carbohydrate.

800 g (1 lb 12 oz) tin apple pie fruit

1 tbs caster (superfine) sugar

250 g (9 oz/1⅔ cups) strawberries, hulled and sliced

75 g (2¾ oz/¾ cup) rolled oats

60 g (2¼ oz/⅓ cup) soft brown sugar

85 g (3 oz/½ cup) wholemeal (wholewheat) plain (all-purpose) flour

1 tbs pepitas (pumpkin seeds)

50 g (1¾ oz) cold butter, chopped

low-fat vanilla or strawberry yoghurt, to serve

Prep time: 10 minutes

Cooking time: 15 minutes

Serves 4–6

Preheat the oven to 180°C (350°F/Gas 4). Place the apples in a 1.5 litre (52 fl oz/6 cup), deep 20 x 5 cm (8 x 2 in) ovenproof dish. Sprinkle with the sugar and stir through the strawberries.

Combine the rolled oats, sugar, flour and pepitas in a bowl. Rub in the butter, using the fingertips, until crumbly. Do not overmix. Spread evenly over the apple. Bake for 15–20 minutes, or until golden brown. Serve with the yoghurt.

nutrition per serve (6) Energy 1210 kJ (288 Cal); Fat 9.2 g; Carbohydrate 45.6 g; Protein 4.5 g

pancakes with berry compote

These carb-rich pancakes are great for breakfast, brunch or dessert. The berries add fibre and antioxidants and provide the daily requirement of vitamin C.

125 g (4½ oz/1 cup) plain (all-purpose) flour

1 tbs baking powder

2 tbs caster (superfine) sugar

pinch of salt

250 ml (9 fl oz/1 cup) skim or no-fat milk

2 eggs, beaten

30 g (1 oz) butter, melted

½ tsp vanilla essence

oil spray

250 g (9 oz/1¼ cups) strawberries, hulled, quartered

125 g (4½ oz/¾ cup) fresh or frozen blueberries

170 g (5¾ oz/¾ cup) caster (superfine) sugar

3 tbs lemon juice

125 g (4½ oz/¾ cup) fresh or frozen raspberries

125 g (4½ oz/¾ cup) fresh or frozen blackberries

Prep time: 10 minutes
Cooking time: 25 minutes
Serves 6

Sift the flour, baking powder, sugar and a pinch of salt into a bowl. Whisk together the milk, egg, butter and vanilla essence in a separate bowl. Whisk the milk mixture into the flour mixture until a smooth batter is formed.

Heat and spray a large, non-stick frying pan with the oil. Pour in 2 tablespoons of batter, 4 batches at a time, and cook for 2 minutes, or until bubbles appear. Turn over and cook on the other side. Makes 24 pancakes altogether.

Put the strawberries, blueberries, sugar and lemon juice in a saucepan and cook over a medium heat for 2 minutes, or until the sugar has dissolved and the berries release their juices.

Remove from the heat and stir in the raspberries and blackberries. Serve warm with the pancakes.

nutrition per serve Energy 1359 kJ (324 Cal); Fat 6.3 g; Carbohydrate 58.1 g; Protein 7.5 g

spiced creamed rice with apricots

A delicious low-fat dessert or breakfast, rich in carbohydrate, potassium and beta-carotene. Just the thing for topping up your fuel tanks.

24 dried apricot halves

750 ml (26 fl oz/3 cups) skim milk

110 g (3¾ oz/½ cup) arborio rice

1 vanilla pod, split lengthways

¼ tsp ground nutmeg

pinch ground cardamom

2 tsp caster (superfine) sugar

170 g (6 oz/¾ cup) sugar

2 cinnamon sticks

2 tsp grated orange zest

3 tbs orange juice

Prep time: 10 minutes + 30 minutes soaking
Cooking time: 50 minutes
Serves 4–6

Put the apricots in a heatproof bowl, cover with boiling water and leave to soak for 30 minutes, or until the apricots are plump.

Pour the milk into a saucepan, add the rice, vanilla pod, nutmeg and cardamom and bring to the boil. Reduce the heat and simmer gently, stirring frequently, for 25 minutes, or until the rice is soft and creamy and has absorbed most of the milk. Remove from the heat.

Remove the vanilla pod, scrape out the seeds and mix them back into the rice. Stir in the caster sugar.

Meanwhile, to make the sugar syrup put the sugar, cinnamon sticks, orange zest and juice in a saucepan with 600 ml (21 fl oz/2½ cups) water. Bring to the boil, then reduce the heat and simmer for 10 minutes. Drain the apricots and add to the pan. Return to the boil, then reduce the heat to low and simmer for 5 minutes, or until soft. Remove the apricots with a slotted spoon. Return the sauce to the boil, then boil until reduced by half. Remove from the heat, cool a little and pour over the apricots. Serve the apricots with the creamed rice.

nutrition per serve (6) Energy 1079 kJ (257 Cal); Fat 0.3 g; Carbohydrate 57.9 g; Protein 6.6 g

lemon grass & ginger fruit salad

This refreshing blend of tropical fruit is a good source of fibre, vitamin C, potassium and other antioxidants. Serve with low-fat yoghurt for a calcium boost.

55 g (2 oz/¼ cup) caster (superfine) sugar

2 x 2 cm (¾ x ¾ in) piece fresh ginger, thinly sliced

1 stem lemon grass, bruised and halved

pulp from 1 large passionfruit

1 Fiji red pawpaw

½ honeydew melon

1 large mango

1 small pineapple

12 fresh lychees

1 large handful mint, shredded, to serve

Prep time: 20 minutes

Cooking time: 10 minutes

Serves 4

Place the sugar, ginger and lemon grass in a small saucepan, add 125 ml (4 fl oz/½ cup) water and stir over a low heat to dissolve the sugar. Boil for 5 minutes, or until reduced to 80 ml (2½ fl oz/⅓ cup or about 4 tablespoons), then set aside to cool. Strain the syrup and add the passionfruit pulp.

Peel and seed the pawpaw and melon. Cut the pawpaw and the melon into 4 cm (1½ in) cubes. Peel the mango and cut the flesh into cubes, discarding the stone. Peel, halve and core the pineapple and cut into cubes. Peel the lychees, then make a slit in the flesh and remove the seed.

Place all the fruit in a large serving bowl. Pour over the syrup, or serve separately, if preferred. Garnish with the mint.

HINT: *If fresh lychees are not available, you can use tinned ones.*

nutrition per serve Energy 1146 kJ (273 Cal); Fat 1 g; Carbohydrate 58.2 g; Protein 4.2 g

The key to performing well is to eat well. With so much precious time reserved for training, it can seem impossible to fit in any time for cooking. But once you know the basics of good nutrition and stock up your kitchen with great ingredients, it's easy to eat healthy foods every day. There is also a great range of easy, ready-made commercial products that you can keep on hand for when hunger strikes.

useful information & index

plan to eat well

SHOPPING TIPS

• *Take a shopping list with you for easy reference.*

• *Purchase different-sized storage containers for storing and freezing foods.*

• *Take advantage of time-saving products, such as ready-made low-fat sauces, grated low-fat cheeses and pre-cut and pre-trimmed meats.*

• *Read the nutrition panel on food labels.*

• *Buy a wide range of ingredients so that your meals are varied and interesting.*

If you're serious about improving your health it's important to have ready access to a range of healthy foods. It's easier to eat a nutritious diet if you take time each week to make sure that your pantry, fridge and freezer are well stocked with healthy foods and ingredients for nutritious meals that can be made quickly. Reserve some time each weekend to cook up large batches of your favourite low-fat meals that you can freeze in portions and then defrost for meals during the week. A microwave is also a great investment for reheating and preparing meals quickly.

foods for the freezer

Bread, pizza bases, English muffins, bagels, fruit loaf, filo pastry, skinless chicken fillets, fish fillets, marinara mix, lean meat, frozen vegetables, frozen vegetable stir-fry mixes, thick-cut, 97% fat-free oven fries, grated reduced-fat cheese, frozen berries, sorbet, gelato, low-fat frozen fruit dessert.

foods for the fridge

Fresh fruit and vegetables, juices, mineral water, reduced-or low-fat dairy products or soy alternatives (milk, cheese, yoghurt, custard), smoked salmon, reduced-fat margarine, eggs, reduced-fat deli meat slices, fresh pasta (ravioli, tortellini, lasagne sheets), fresh Asian noodles, pasta sauce, minced herbs, lemon juice, tomato paste, mustard, fat-free dressings, linseed meal.

foods for the pantry

Bread, low-fat crispbreads and crackers, rice cakes, natural muesli, breakfast cereals, porridge oats, low-fat breakfast cereal bars, rice, pasta, noodles, tinned spaghetti, couscous, polenta, low-fat muffin and pancake mixes, dried fruit, nuts and seeds, wheat germ, oat bran, potatoes, low-fat microwave popcorn, low-fat pretzels, tinned legumes (lentils, beans, baked beans, chickpeas), tinned tomatoes, tinned fish in brine or water, bottled pasta sauces, low-fat casserole/cook-in sauces, long life reduced- or low-fat milk, soy sauce, oyster sauce, vinegar, dried herbs and spices, stock cubes or long-life stocks, low-fat soups (tinned, sachets, packets), baking ingredients (flour, sugar, etc), spray oils (olive and canola), vegemite, marmite, fruit spreads, honey, low-fat drinking chocolate mixes.

the healthy diet pyramid

EAT LEAST
sugar, fats and oils, salt

EAT IN MODERATION
eggs, dairy products and
alternatives, meat, poultry, fish,
seafood and nuts

EAT MOST
grains and cereal products,
fruits, vegetables, legumes

index

Published by Murdoch Books Pty Limited.

Chief Executive: Juliet Rogers
Publisher: Kay Scarlett

Editorial Director: Diana Hill
Project Manager: Zoë Harpham
Creative Director: Marylouise Brammer
Design Concept and Design: Susanne Geppert
Editor: Carla Holt
Food Editor: Michelle Earl
Photographer: Ian Hofstetter
Stylist: Jane Collins
Food preparation: Joanne Kelly
Recipes: Michelle Earl and the Murdoch Books Test Kitchen
Production: Monika Vidovic

National Library of Australia Cataloguing-in-Publication Data: Holt, Susanna. Fitness Food. Includes index. ISBN 1 74045 362 X. 1. Athletes–nutrition. 2. Physical fitness—nutritional aspects. I. Title. (Series: Food for fitness series). 613.2024796.

Printed by Toppan Hong Kong. PRINTED IN CHINA. First published 2004.

Murdoch Books Australia
Pier 8/9, 23 Hickson Road
Millers Point NSW 2000
Phone: + 61 (0) 2 8220 2000 Fax: + 61 (0) 2 8220 2558

Murdoch Books UK Ltd
Erico House, 6th Floor North, 93–99 Upper Richmond Road
Putney, London SW15 2TG
Phone: + 44 (0) 20 8785 5995   Fax +44 (0) 20 8785 5985

IMPORTANT: Those who might be at risk from the effects of salmonella food poisoning (the elderly, pregnant women, young children and those suffering from immune-deficiency diseases) should consult their doctor with any concerns about eating raw eggs.

NUTRITIONAL ANALYSIS: The nutritional information given for each recipe does not include any optional ingredients or accompaniments, such as rice or pasta, unless they are included in specific quantities in the ingredients list. The nutritional values are approximations and can be affected by biological and seasonal variations in foods, the unknown composition of some manufactured foods and uncertainty in the dietary database. Nutrient data given are derived primarily from the AUSNUT 2001 database produced by Food Standards Australia New Zealand. The number of serves listed per recipe is an average only and may not be representative of the number of serves that a very active male would obtain from a dish (for example, they may get fewer serves from the same dish than a smaller female).

CONVERSION GUIDE: You may find cooking times vary depending on the oven you are using. For fan-forced ovens, as a general rule, set the oven temperature to 20°C (70°F) lower than indicated in the recipe. We have used 20 ml (4 teaspoon) tablespoon measures. If you are using a 15 ml (3 teaspoon) tablespoon, for most recipes the difference will not be noticeable. However, for recipes using baking powder, gelatine, bicarbonate of soda, small amounts of flour and cornflour (cornstarch), add an extra teaspoon for each tablespoon specified.

The Publisher thanks Dinosaur Designs and Mud Australia for the assistance in the photography of this book.